THE BEST
FRONT RANGE
BIRD
HIKES

Western bluebird at nest cavity

COLORADO
MOUNTAIN CLUB
GUIDEBOOK

THE BEST
FRONT RANGE
BIRD
HIKES

NORM LEWIS

The Colorado Mountain Club Press
Golden, Colorado

The Best Front Range Bird Hikes
© 2021 Norm Lewis

PUBLISHED BY

The Colorado Mountain Club Press
710 10th Street, Suite 200, Golden, Colorado 80401
303-996-2743 I email: cmcpress@cmc.org I website: http://www.cmcpress.org

Founded in 1912, The Colorado Mountain Club is the largest outdoor recreation, education, and conservation organization in the Rocky Mountains. Look for our books at your local bookstore or outdoor retailer, or online at www.cmcpress.org.

CORRECTIONS: We greatly appreciate when readers alert us to errors or outdated information by contacting us at cmcpress@cmc.org.

Norm Lewis: author and photographer
Erika K. Arroyo: designer
Elle Klock: copyeditor

Cover photo: Pine grosbeak

DISTRIBUTED TO THE BOOK TRADE BY
Mountaineers Books
1001 SW Klickitat Way, Suite 201, Seattle, WA 98134, 800-553-4453
www.mountaineersbooks.org

We gratefully acknowledge the financial support of the people of Colorado through the Scientific and Cultural Facilities District of greater metropolitan Denver for our publishing activities.

TOPOGRAPHIC MAPS created with Gaia GPS software.

Printed in the United States of America

21 / 10 9 8 7 6 5 4 3 2 1

ISBN 978-1-937052-56-0

ACKNOWLEDGMENTS

I would like to thank several people for their invaluable assistance and support for the completion of this book.

Right at the top of the list is Frank Burzynski, who originated the idea for the book, supplied many suggestions for hikes, provided several photographs, and demonstrated admirable patience as I toiled up several trails in his accomplished wake. Others who provided company and encouragement (often in the form of pointing and laughing) on many hikes are Ted Cooper, Rod Mahaffey, Gary Potter (hey, wanna do Chicago Lakes tomorrow?), Nina Routh, and Mike Serruto.

Thanks also to my editor, Sarah Gorecki, who stepped in after many stops, starts, and changes to help me drag this project to the finish line!

DEDICATION

To my beloved wife, Debbie, who has spent many a day at home wondering where the heck her husband is and when he might next appear. And to our two patient little dogs, Griz and the late, much-missed Panda (who crossed the Rainbow Bridge as I was finishing this project), who also waited at home wondering when Dad would return to get back to his primary responsibility, namely, doing something for the pups.

Rabbit Mountain in autumn

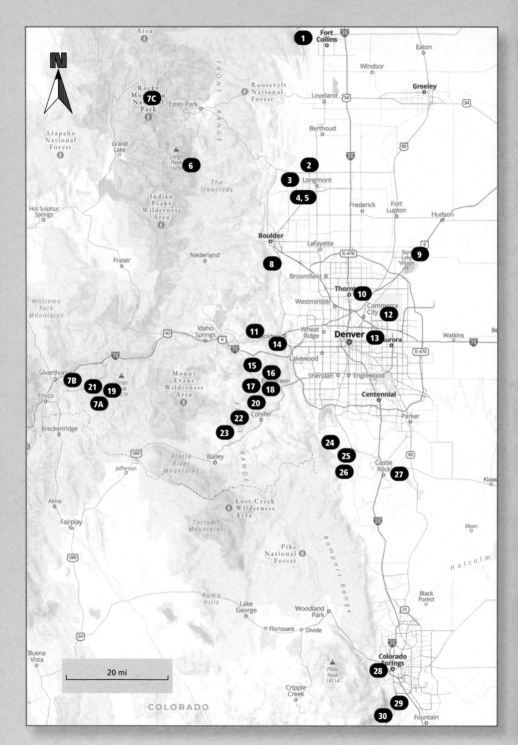

AREA MAP

Contents

INTRODUCTION

Two of the most popular and fastest-growing outdoor activities in Colorado and across the U.S. are hiking and birding (formerly referred to as "bird-watching," a term that is outdated and not generally used by birders today). There are hundreds of books detailing hikes of every description and field guides to assist in locating and identifying birds, but there have been few attempts at combining the two. The purpose of this book is to supply a resource for hikers who would like to add another dimension to their treks, and for birders who wish to combine birding with additional physical activity.

Birding and hiking seem similar and naturally complementary, but closer examination reveals that this is not necessarily the case. In fact, the two are at cross-purposes with each other. The hiker tends to be destination oriented; while stopping occasionally along the trail to enjoy the surroundings, the hiker has an endpoint in mind and hastens to reach it. The birder, on the other hand, places no value on speed and, in fact, finds haste a deterrent to their goal of finding and identifying as many bird species as possible.

Another difference between hiking and birding is quality of scenery and surroundings. While there is a great degree of overlap in this regard between the two disciplines, there are also some distinct differences. A hiker will insist that their route include some attractive vistas and appealing landscapes. Since birders are, in general, also fans of the outdoors, their wishes would be similar—but not always. There are many notable birding sites that would not make anyone's vacation wish list. Birders pass many a pleasurable hour observing the denizens of dumps and water treatment plants. A notable example in Colorado is the Larimer County Landfill, a giant trash heap that stands in stark contrast to the nearby mountains. However, the landfill has for the past several years hosted a visiting gyrfalcon in winter, resulting in the area being overrun not only with garbage trucks, but also hopeful birders. Perhaps the most famous of these odoriferous destinations is the Brownsville Dump in the Lower Rio Grande Valley of Texas. For many years (but unfortunately no longer) the dump was known as the only place in North America to see the Tamaulipas (formerly Mexican) crow. So many birders made the journey to see this bird that the dump considerably set aside a special "birder area," which provided a safe haven from the roaring dump trucks, if not from the smell.

In this volume, we will join birding and hiking into a single entity, which combines some of the most enjoyable aspects of each. We will offer some helpful information for the experienced hiker who wants to add bird observation and identification to their skills, and suggest a variety of hikes for birders that feature the potential for interesting bird sightings. Finding such sites in Colorado is not challenging; gorgeous scenery is everywhere, as are birds. Unless you are a big fan of architecture, downtown Denver has little to offer in the way of scenery, but even there we find birds. Yes, there are a lot of pigeons, but the fortunate observer may also see one of the urban peregrine falcons that prey upon them!

This presents us with a challenge: what shall we call our participant in this hiking and birding enterprise? Hiking-birder and birding-hiker seem too awkward. Combining the two yields a couple of promising possibilities, but "biker" has obvious shortcomings: are we referring to an individual careening down the trail on a mountain bike, or to a large bearded fellow carrying binoculars and riding a Harley? No, "biker" won't work. The other option is "hirder," although this presents the misleading possibility that sheep might somehow be involved. The inclusion of the "i," however, should allay those concerns, so "hirder" might work, at least for the purposes of this book. We don't expect the term to attain any kind of widespread popularity . . . or perhaps we will just stick with "hiker" and assume that the reader understands we are referring to a hiker who is interested in birds.

WHY BIRDING?

If you ask a dozen birders why they love birding, you will probably get a dozen different answers. For some, it is the beauty of birds. Some are interested in bird vocalizations while others study migration. For others, it is fascination with avian behaviors. The seemingly endless variety of forms, functions, and habitats that comprise the world of birds supplies a source of wonder and amazement that no birder can ever exhaust. Colorado has a sufficient variety of birds and their habitats to keep even the most enthusiastic birder busy for a lifetime. We will attempt in this book to give samples of as many habitats (and the wide variety of birds who inhabit them) as possible within the Front Range and adjacent foothills. The hiker who completes every hike described here will have had an opportunity to see virtually every regularly occurring bird species that the Front Range has to offer—and to see them in settings of undeniable beauty, as well as scientific interest.

It is worth noting that in describing hikes for birding, the author immediately encounters several problems in trying to give the reader the best possible information. These problems include seasonal variation, migration(s), elevation, and geographic distribution. Obviously, in a climate with temperature swings as dramatic as those found in Colorado, many birds will be present only in certain seasons. There is overlap, but we have sizable populations of birds that are here only in winter, summer, or migration. And for those migratory species, the puzzle is more complicated than "here in the summer, gone south in the winter." Raptors, for example, migrate earlier than songbirds. Sandhill cranes pass through Colorado almost entirely in March, but may be seen returning south for several months in the autumn as they undertake their more relaxed fall migration. And then there is the issue of what I like to refer to as the "double migration," which is one part horizontal and one part vertical. Many birds arrive in spring from the south and linger at lower elevations to feed and prepare for mating and nesting, then proceed up in elevation.

There are many species that show up in the plains in April and May, only to disappear from the lowlands as they move up to their nesting ranges in the mountains. An excellent example is the yellow-rumped warbler. In early May, it seems that every tree in the plains has several. By June, they are gone. They are also one of the migrant songbirds most likely to be found in winter. Other species nest at higher elevations and return lower in the winter, but do not have a "horizontal" component to their migration; they just show up in greater numbers in the near plains. American dipper and Townsend's solitaire are two examples. I have attempted to address geographic distribution by including hikes from all along the Front Range, from Fort Collins to Colorado Springs. There are a number of species that may be seen on our more southern hikes that are rarely found to the north: canyon towhee and Bewick's wren, for example.

NOTE: The hikes in this book are presented in roughly north-to-south order.

As we wander the many trails and treks of the Colorado Front Range, we should be mindful of the fact that neither we, nor our hiking and adventuring predecessors, are the first to pass this way. Long before Europeans appeared on the scene, this was the homeland of many Indigenous peoples. In addition to the Apache, Kiowa, and Navajo who called the lands that would someday be known as Colorado home, the Ute, Cheyenne, Arapahoe, and Comanche people inhabited the very lands upon which we walk. It should not be forgotten that the people who were here before us—and who still live in Colorado—were forcefully removed from the magnificent landscapes that we enjoy today.

Finally, it can be helpful to be aware of scientific taxonomic names for the birds. Knowing these can help organize and identify birds by family characteristics. However, since birds, unlike plants and some other flora and fauna, are universally called by one distinct common name, in this volume we will confine ourselves to common names only. By whatever names birds are called, their impact on our lives on many levels is undeniable. So, I encourage you to get out there and enjoy these hikes for birds. Catalog them as you wish, call them whatever you care to, but get out there!

BIRDING TIPS

There are a number of techniques that might assist the hiker in finding and observing more birds. Many of these are obvious, but I will list a few that might be helpful.

    Adjusting the diopter of your binoculars. This procedure is important yet frequently overlooked. The purpose of the diopter is to adapt your binoculars to your specific vision. If not adjusted, the focus will be off to some degree and you will not realize the full potential of your optics. Begin by locating the diopter on your binoculars; it is most often the right eyepiece. Find something to use as a cover for each barrel of the binocular. If you have the covers for the lenses, one of these will do nicely. Assuming that the right eyepiece is the diopter, cover the right barrel and find an object at middle distance on which to focus. I prefer a sign or something with writing on it, but any object will do. Use the main focus mechanism to bring the view through the left eyepiece into sharp focus. Remove the cover from the right barrel and place it over the left. Look through the right side and use the diopter to bring that side into focus. Remove the cover. The view through the binocular should now be adjusted for your eyes and the image should be sharp.

Motion. Birds are sensitive to movement and your behavior should be adjusted accordingly. Of course, some species are more skittish than others; red crossbills will often feed on the ground and let an observer walk right up to them, while a Virginia rail will flee into the cattails at the slightest indication of movement. In general, it is best to attempt to observe with as little movement as possible. Do your best, but good luck with that. Many birds will run you around their tree multiple times before flying into the next county. One way to keep from flushing the bird is to, as much as possible, bird from the shade or shadows. Harsh lighting intensifies movement, so staying out of sun will ameliorate this. An additional technique that can aid in keeping a bird from flushing is to approach it indirectly, by either zig-zagging toward it or spiraling in. In any case, walking directly toward a bird (or any wildlife, for that matter) can be interpreted as a threat, and may result in a gone bird.

More on motion and bird location. Some birding guides will discourage their participants from pointing at birds because the sudden raising of the arm can spook them (the bird, not the birder). Good luck with that, too. I have attempted to wean myself from the habit of pointing, to no avail. Apparently, it is an addiction with which most birders are afflicted. However, when you are birding with companions, you will need to develop techniques for helping get them on the bird you just found. Failure to do so can result in the termination of a friendship, or perhaps even your life, depending upon the rarity of the bird. From my experience, many birders are terrible at giving directions to a bird in the field. Jumping up and down and shouting, "It's in the green tree!" is ineffective. One popular technique to address this problem is the "clock face" method. Rather than jumping up and down and shouting, try using the tree (or bush, or shrub, or whatever) as a clock face. Give the time position and then a distance in from the edge of the tree. "The cerulean warbler is at two o'clock, three feet in," gives your companions a good opportunity to find the bird and for you to escape their ire at missing a potential life species. In the case of a tall skinny tree (like many conifers), a distance from the top or bottom of the tree, and which side of the tree the bird is on, can be helpful.

Norm's Geographic Method. OK, that might sound a little self-important, but I have found that using this simple method (which I probably didn't invent, but will be happy to take credit for) can help birders, especially beginners, to become more efficient at getting a good look at a bird, once the birder has the bird's general location. I started teaching this technique after hearing complaints from fellow birders, often sounding something like, "I know where the bird is, but I can't get on the damned thing!" or something more colorful. Here's how it works: once you have detected bird movement or have a pretty good idea where the bird is, do not immediately start scanning for the bird, which is frequently buried in a leafy tree or bush. Instead, find an easily locatable nearby geographic location. This can be almost anything: a dead leaf, a splash of sunlight, a patch of bark, an odd-shaped branch. Quickly note the location of the bird relative to your mark and locate the mark in your binoculars. From there it is easy to find the bird: six inches to the left, a foot above, or whatever. Scanning across a uniformly colored tree, looking for the movement you just saw with the unaided eye, can be a lot trickier than it sounds.

Record keeping. This is a subject that can create a little controversy. Is there a hobby out there that doesn't include factions that stake out positions and create internal friction? Maybe stamp collecting? Well, birding is no different, and listing is a topic that comes up frequently. Some birders record every sighting from every outing and carefully tend their ABA (American Birding Association) life list, state lists, county lists, yard lists, international lists, and every other imaginable list. At the other end of the spectrum are those who record nothing and insist birding should be done for the sheer enjoyment of watching the birds, without making a record-keeping marathon of it. So, what is the correct way to do this? Any way you care to! That is one of the beauties of birding; it can be tailored to your specific preferences and practiced any way you please, within the bounds of proper ethics. And that applies in spades to record keeping. If you wish to keep records of your sightings, there are many ways to do it. There is the old-fashioned way of paper and pencil. That works just fine, but after a few years you will find yourself submerged in piles of paper. Unless your ambitions include becoming a professional bookkeeper, this situation can become unmanageable. The solution, of course, is computerized records. Which leads to the next question: how? There are many bird listing programs available for purchase, but I recommend using *eBird Mobile*, the bird listing program developed at the Cornell Lab of Ornithology. The lab can be found at birds.cornell.edu and the program at ebird.org. Using *eBird* is a win-win for birders and birds. First, it is free! Just sign up and start entering data. It gives you an opportunity to participate in "citizen science," in that all data entered into *eBird* is shared with the Cornell Lab and is used extensively in research. Second, *eBird* keeps all your records, with no need for any additional effort on your part. Enter your sightings from each birding outing on the *eBird* mobile app for your cell phone and *eBird* will do the rest for you. All your data will be compiled on the main *eBird* site. ABA life list? No problem. County list? Foreign county list? State list? Yard list? All right there. And did I mention, it's free?

Photography. Taking photos of your sightings can fulfill several purposes. Some like to revisit great experiences through their photos. Some like to share photos via a variety of social networks. Some enjoy the art of bird photography. These days if you submit a sighting of a rare bird, you will probably want to have photo documentation with it. Whatever the motivation, in recent years photography has added a whole new element to birding. So, no matter whether you use a $10,000 professional setup or a point-and-shoot, enjoy taking your photos and share them however you choose, or not. There are still birders who aren't interested in hauling around a camera and would rather just look at the birds. And as with all things birding, you get to do it however you please!

ON HIKING AND BIRDING

For those who consider themselves primarily hikers, there is little mystery to their pastime: go to the trailhead, walk up the trail to the end, enjoy the scenery along the way. Rinse, repeat. That is, turn around and go back, or complete the loop. It's straightforward. However, if you have decided to add birding to your outing, things are about to change profoundly.

First, your direct route to the top (or bottom, as the case may be) will be interrupted repeatedly by those annoying feathered miscreants. They seem to be everywhere and nowhere. You may walk for a mile and see nothing but the afore-mentioned scenery, then suddenly find yourself surrounded by motion and sound. This is one of the great attractions/frustrations of birding: its unpredictability. For example, every hike in this book has been chosen to provide an opportunity to see a particular species of bird (and in most cases entire suites of birds), yet there are no guarantees. Perhaps you will achieve wonderful sightings, perhaps you will see nothing at all. The results are usually somewhere in between, depending upon the energy expended and the skills of the observer.

The challenge always lies in the absence of any certainty. I remember a long-ago winter outing. I debated as to a destination and decided that a drive across Guanella Pass could potentially be productive. There are lots of places along the way to stop, look, and listen, one of which is included in Ptarmigan Ptrio (Chapter 7). So, I hurried up I-70 to Georgetown, turned off on Guanella Pass Road, and began the transit across the pass. A couple of hours and twenty-three miles later, I arrived at Grant. Along the way, I had seen nothing, not a single bird. I suppose there is something comforting about knowing that your worst birding day ever (at least in terms of species seen) is behind you, but that is little consolation for the birder who has invested a day into an area and come up completely empty—but that is the nature of the game.

Next, you will be dogged by the desire for knowledge and information. It is inherent in the nature of birding that however much you know, it is never enough. This leads inevitably to the acquisition of field guides, bird-finding guides, books on bird families (owls, woodpeckers, warblers, ducks, and so on, ad infinitum), species accounts, birding stories, and magazine subscriptions. You will join the American Birding Association, the Cornell Lab of Ornithology and other organizations, and you will receive their magazines and newsletters. Your newfound desire for information will make it seem downright tragic to dispose of any of this material, even though you realize you can never read it all. The books and magazines begin to accumulate into unmanageable mountains. Your spouse threatens divorce. So remember, this pursuit of knowledge can have consequences.

EQUIPMENT

As with many activities, hiking and birding can be accomplished with a range of equipment, from simple and inexpensive to sophisticated and pricey. Hiking requires only sturdy footwear, a water bottle, and sunscreen. Birding, on the other hand, ups the equipment ante. The most obvious addition is a good pair of binoculars. A serviceable pair can be purchased for a couple hundred dollars while the top brands can run into the thousands. Many birders also choose to include a camera in their equipment array, which adds expense.

These days most folks have a cell phone, which has become more of a necessity than an option. Many hikers have been rescued via a cell call from some lonely mountainside. For birding, the use of *eBird Mobile* (discussed under "Birding Tips") has become widespread. Just as record keeping is popular among birders, there are numerous apps that allow the hiker to record their track for posterity.

Clothing is another accessory that should not be overlooked. First, be sure to wear some; the authorities still frown on birding without clothing in most locations. Assuming you have that issue under control, there are a number of options you should consider, depending upon the circumstances. While outerwear is obvious, your gear should begin with a good hat. Ballcaps have been the go-to headwear for birders for years, but wide-brimmed chapeaus that protect the ears and neck, as well as the face and eyes, have been gaining in popularity. From there, the rest of the birder/hiker wardrobe is straightforward, with a lot of options. A heavy coat and some kind of heavy lined pants are a must in winter, of course. A birder standing on the shore at Barr Lake on a windy day in January will much appreciate remembering to add long underwear to their outfit. Likewise, a thick pair of wool socks and heavy waterproof (emphasis on *waterproof*) boots will be a great benefit. A fleece jacket can also be a welcome addition to your winter layers. For summer birding, especially in warmer climes, a light breathable cotton or nylon shirt should be adequate. Nylon zip-off pants are popular and heavy winter boots can be set aside in favor of light walking shoes or even sturdy sandals.

If you are stocking your car with equipment for all seasons and situations, you might want to include a pair of Wellingtons or irrigation boots for those occasions when wading through sloppy terrain becomes necessary. Keeping a change of socks and shoes is a good idea for when you do the above without benefit of waterproof footwear.

And, of course, most birders want access to an identification resource in the field. There are a number of good field guides, but arguably the best for carrying on birding outings is the *National Geographic Field Guide to the Birds of North America*. The *Geo Guide* has gone through many editions and, due to the changes in taxonomic order, name changes, and splitting of species, it is best to have a newer version that reflects all this nomenclature juggling. Another fine choice is *The Sibley Guide to Birds*. The *Sibley* is larger than the *Geo Guide* and not as convenient to carry around. However, while the *Geo Guide* is long on information and somewhat shorter on illustrations, the *Sibley* is just the opposite, making them complementary to each other. In my guide-carrying days, I kept a *Geo Guide* with me and a *Sibley* in my vehicle for cross-referencing. However, these days I have come to rely upon field guide apps. There is an excellent *Sibley* app, and *iBird Pro Guide to Birds* is also popular.

Along the trail, above tree line in Rocky Mountain National Park

Chapter 1. Lory State Park

ROUND-TRIP DISTANCE	8.5 miles
ELEVATION GAIN	1,600 feet
MAX ELEVATION	6,850 feet
TRAIL TYPE	Combination out-and-back, loop
DIFFICULTY	Strenuous
BEST SEASON(S)	Late spring, summer

FEATURED BIRDS: Cordilleran flycatcher; Say's phoebe; western and eastern kingbird; loggerhead and northern shrike; warbling vireo; white-breasted nuthatch; blue-gray gnatcatcher; mountain bluebird; gray catbird; Virginia's, MacGillivray's, and Wilson's warblers; yellow-breasted chat; spotted and green-tailed towhees; black-headed grosbeak; lazuli bunting; western meadowlark; Bullock's oriole; dusky grouse; northern goshawk; northern pygmy-owl; northern saw-whet owl; Hammond's flycatcher; Steller's jay; pygmy and red-breasted nuthatches; brown creeper; ruby-crowned and golden-crowned kinglets; western bluebird; Townsend's solitaire; dark-eyed junco; western tanager; Cassin's finch; red crossbill; and evening grosbeak

COMMENT: Lory State Park is situated in the low foothills on the west side of Horsetooth Reservoir, on the west side of Fort Collins. Our outing in the state park is, to paraphrase Charles Dickens, a tale of two journeys. The first half of our hike, on the Timber Trail, passes through foothill scrublands featuring vast tracts of mountain mahogany punctuated with thickets of shrubs and an occasional ponderosa pine, plus a creek with riparian habitat. At roughly the halfway point, the trail gains sufficient elevation to enter coniferous forest. The forest is divided into two sub-habitats: on sunny south-facing slopes, open ponderosa woodland dominates, while wetter north-facing slopes are covered in spruce-fir. Of course, each hosts its own suite of birds. Our return route down the Well Gulch Nature Trail will pass through riparian habitat and add a suite of birds not seen elsewhere on the trails.

GETTING THERE: Take I-25 to Exit 269 (CO Highway 14) and go west on 14 (Mulberry St.) for 3.3 miles to Riverside. Go right for a mile and turn right again on Highway 287 (College Ave.). Go north for three and a half miles as 287 curves to the west. At the traffic circle, take the second exit and continue west on Roads 52E and 54G for 2.7 miles, and make a slight left on Rist Canyon Road. In a mile, go left on

Road 23 and go south for 1.4 miles, and turn right on Road 25G. In 1.6 miles, you will enter the park, and shortly see a turnoff on the right to the Timber Trail/West Valley Trail parking lot.

THE ROUTE: Before starting out, check the little drainage on the north side of the parking lot. In the early morning, this little brushy woodland can be alive with the songs of house wrens, song sparrows, goldfinches, spotted towhees, and more. Having checked the draw, walk across the lot and start up the Timber Trail to the left. For the next two miles the habitat is about as monocultural as you will find anywhere this side of the sagebrush plains of northwest Colorado. The dominant flora is mountain mahogany and the birds are those that are found in brushy foothills prairies. On an early spring morning, the songs of western meadowlarks,

Williamson's sapsucker

Horsetooth Reservoir from the trail

western kingbirds, and spotted towhees fill the air, and can be almost deafening. You will never be out of earshot of the spotted towhees. With a little luck, there may be a green-tailed towhee mixed in with the ubiquitous spotteds.

As you cross this long, winding stretch of brushy habitat, watch also for Say's phoebe, mountain bluebird, blue-gray gnatcatcher, Woodhouse's scrub-jay, and Swainson's and red-tailed hawks. At the 2.1-mile mark you will pass the intersection with the Kimmons Trail, which could serve as a descent, though our route makes a different choice. In another quarter mile is Well Gulch Nature Trail, which we will use later, but for now, continue on the Timber Trail. At 2.4 miles there is a small footbridge. From here our route will follow multiple switchbacks as the trail gains elevation. As you climb, watch and listen for birds typical of this mixed ponderosa and spruce-fir forest, including pygmy, white-breasted, and red-breasted nuthatches; Steller's jay; dark-eyed junco; plumbeous vireo; and chipping sparrow. Continue up Timber Trail to its intersection with Westridge Trail. The open ponderosa forest here hosts red crossbill, western bluebird, and downy and hairy woodpeckers. Watch cavities in dead trees for nesting pygmy nuthatches and violet-green swallows.

Western bluebird perched high atop a dead ponderosa

From this point, you can follow the Westridge Trail to the south end of the park or take the Arthur's

Rock Trail to Arthur's Rock, and then down to the complex of trails at the south end. For our route, we will return down the Timber Trail, revisit the switchbacks, and look for more birds of the spruce-fir forest.

To complete the hike, first go back down Timber Trail to the switchbacks, and follow them down to the footbridge. Cross the bridge and look for the Well Gulch Nature Trail on the right. Rather than return via the Timber Trail and the lengthy stretch of open brushland from our route up, we will take the Well Gulch Trail, which will add a supplement of habitats not present along the rest of the route. A half mile down the Well Gulch Trail it forks. Take it. Just kidding. Follow the left fork for another half mile to its junction with the West Valley Trail, which goes north back to the trailhead and parking lot.

The trail follows a creek that eventually empties into Horsetooth Reservoir. The habitat along the creek is consistent throughout the section our route follows, with more deciduous riparian vegetation that is found elsewhere along the trail. Likewise, the bird species to be found here are typical of those found in foothills riparian habitat, and many are different from those we have seen previously. There are several groups that can be well represented here. In open areas with perches suitable for hunting on the wing, look for western wood-pewee; blue-gray gnatcatcher;

On the trail up in the ponderosa woodlands

Plumbeous vireo

and dusky, least, and Cordilleran flycatchers. Among the willows and moist thickets there might be MacGillivray's and Wilson's warblers and Lincoln's sparrow. The deciduous trees along the creek host western tanager, Bullock's oriole, yellow warbler, warbling vireo, black-headed grosbeak, and lazuli bunting. Check (and listen!) around dense thickets for the bizarre variety of calls coming from yellow-breasted chat, and in the upland brushy areas, Virginia's warblers can be plentiful.

After completing this stretch of the Well Gulch Trail, follow the West Valley Trail for one mile back to the parking lot. The West Valley affords another opportunity to check for birds of arid upland that you might have missed on the way up.

Creek along Well Gulch Nature Trail

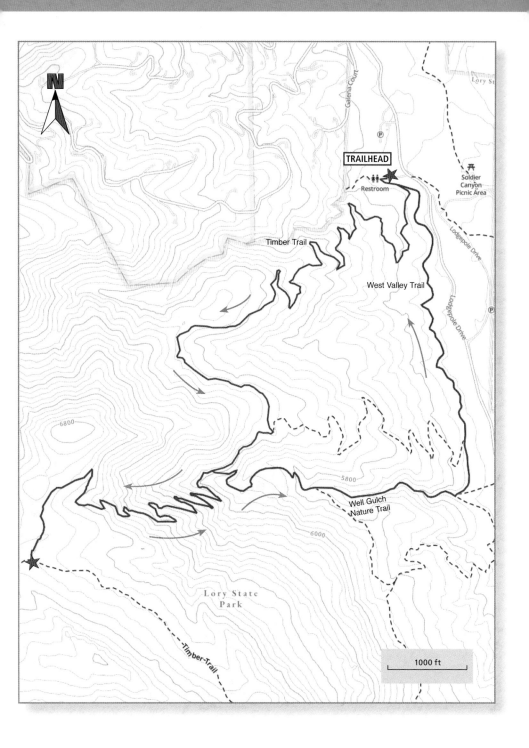

LORY STATE PARK

Chapter 2. **Rabbit Mountain**

ROUND-TRIP DISTANCE	3 miles
ELEVATION GAIN	469 feet
MAX ELEVATION	5,883 feet
TRAIL TYPE	Out-and-back
DIFFICULTY	Easy
BEST SEASON(S)	Early summer

FEATURED BIRDS: Golden eagle; red-tailed, ferruginous, Swainson's, and rough-legged hawks; American kestrel; merlin; prairie and peregrine falcons; northern harrier; Cooper's and sharp-shinned hawks; spotted and green-tailed towhee; rock wren; sage thrasher; blue-gray gnatcatcher; yellow-breasted chat; western meadowlark; Say's phoebe; mountain and western bluebirds; loggerhead and northern shrikes; and blue grosbeak

COMMENT: Rabbit Mountain is a Boulder County Open Space park. There is currently no fee for access. The trail is rocky in places, so sturdy shoes are recommended. I have observed several mountain bikers riding up this trail amid much wobbling and cursing; the same can be true for the unwary hiker. Rabbit Mountain, like the Aiken Canyon hike, is something of a one-trick pony; the habitat for our hike is almost entirely rock outcroppings and hillside scrub, which consists of mountain mahogany and golden currant. The exception is a stand of ponderosa pine near the end of the hike and a few scattered pines along the way, which attract a variety of birds.

GETTING THERE: The turnoff to the Rabbit Mountain Open Space is off CO Highway 66 about a mile east of its intersection with Highway 36, which is about a mile east of downtown Lyons. From Highway 66, turn north on N. 53rd Street, which curves a bit and becomes Vestal Road and then 55th Street. None of this is important, as the road leads north to the open space parking lot with no opportunities for confusion.

THE ROUTE: Our hike begins at the information kiosk at the northeast corner of the parking lot. Follow the Indian Mesa Trail (also referred to as the Eagle Wind Trail on some maps) as it traverses the south face of the mountain. Where there are rocky areas, look for rock wrens, which can be numerous at times in the sum-

Rock wren

Lark sparrow

mer. Spotted towhees are abundant nesters in the brushy patches, and green-tailed towhee can be found here as well. Try to spot sage thrasher and listen for the buzzy calls of blue-gray gnatcatcher.

There are a couple of outlier ponderosa pines along this stretch. Be sure to check these, because as unlikely as it may seem, these isolated trees attract many birds not typical of this general habitat. I have seen such varied species as Bullock's oriole, Virginia's warbler, hairy woodpecker, and cedar waxwing.

Along the trail

There are many open spaces in this sea of brush, so it can be productive to check these for sparrows. Lark sparrows seem to be everywhere at times. Vesper sparrow is also common. White-crowned sparrows and dark-eyed juncos invade in the fall, and American tree sparrow follows in the winter.

As you climb this south-facing slope, do not forget to scan the valley below and the skies above. Blue grosbeak, lazuli bunting, and Say's phoebe can be found in the open prairies. Western meadowlark is also common. The real attraction, however, is the raptor population. The area is known for its variety of raptors. You are almost certain to sight a few. Look for the impressive silhouette of a golden eagle soaring high above. Among the buteos, Swainson's hawk is present in summer and rough-leggeds in winter. Red-tails are common all year. This is also a good place to see the elusive ferruginous hawk. Falcons are well-presented, too, with American kestrel being the most common, but prairie and peregrine are

North hogbacks from the crest of the trail

Cedar waxwing

frequently seen, and a merlin appears occasionally. Cooper's and sharp-shinned hawks are regular.

At the half-mile mark, the Indian Mesa Trail veers to the right and intersects with the Little Thompson Overlook Trail. Our route follows the latter and continues north (left). The trail gradually gains elevation as it winds around the mountain (which more closely resembles a large hill) and continues through hillside scrub habitat. Birds seen here are the same as on earlier parts of the hike. Look for yellow-breasted chat too. Scan the broad swale below and the ridgeline above for cruising northern harrier. Near the terminus of the trail, at around the 1.4-mile mark, you will find an isolated grove of ponderosa pines. These trees are an opportunity

Mountain mahogany

to find pine forest specialties like white- and red-breasted nuthatch, pine siskin, and broad-tailed hummingbird. Semi-rarities have been found here, including brown-capped rosy-finch, evening and pine grosbeaks, golden-crowned kinglet, and band-tailed pigeon.

Just beyond the ponderosa grove is the end of the trail, which, as the name promises, offers sweeping vistas of the surrounding hills and the Little Thompson Valley below. Pause to enjoy your surroundings and then return by the same route to the trailhead.

Sage thrasher

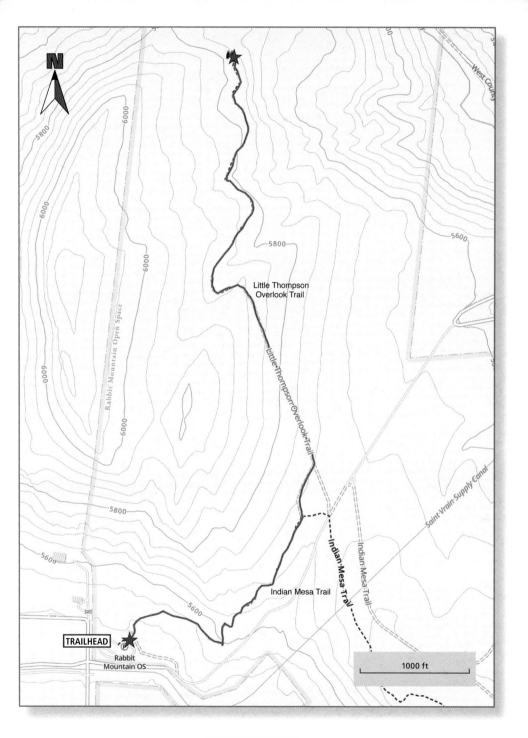

RABBIT MOUNTAIN

Chapter 3. **Old South St. Vrain Road**

ROUND-TRIP DISTANCE	2.1 miles
ELEVATION GAIN	60 feet
MAX ELEVATION	5,450 feet
TRAIL TYPE	Out-and-back
DIFFICULTY	Easy
BEST SEASON(S)	Summer and fall

FEATURED BIRDS: Wild turkeys; corvids, including American crow and common raven, Clark's nutcracker, Steller's and blue jays, and Woodhouse's scrub-jay; white-breasted, red-breasted, and pygmy nuthatches; mountain and black-capped chickadees; house and Cassin's finches; pine siskin; lesser and American goldfinches; house wren; orange-crowned, yellow-rumped, and Wilson's warblers; golden eagle; white-throated swift; Cordilleran flycatcher; canyon wren; violet-green swallow; spotted and green-tailed towhees; black-headed grosbeak; lazuli bunting; American dipper; belted kingfisher; song, white-crowned, Lincoln's, chipping, and fox sparrows; and dark-eyed junco

COMMENT: This hike is actually more of a stroll; it is included in this book for two reasons. First, it is a nice walk that can be alive with a variety of birds. Second, it is a convenient way to add some relaxed walking and numerous species to your day after completing the Rabbit Mountain or Heil Valley Ranch hikes.

The entire route follows the old road that was cut off by construction of the new Highway 7. It is lightly traveled, but the hiker should exercise caution in sharing the road with cars and cyclists.

GETTING THERE: From the east, take Highway 36 through Lyons to the point where it T's with 5th Avenue. Go left (south) on 5th, which becomes CO Highway 7. A half mile from the intersection, turn left on Old South St. Vrain Road.

Cedar waxwing

South St. Vrain Creek

Follow the road for another half mile, until you come to an informal parking area on the right, which is just beyond the last house and before a concrete structure.

THE ROUTE: The geographic setting of this route is rather unique; it features low cliffs on the immediate south side of the road, towering cliffs on the north side of Highway 7, brushy hillsides, a number of sloughs and marshes, and South St. Vrain Creek.

Note that almost all of the featured species listed above can be seen along the road. However, there are a few places that are particularly favorable for some. There are often wild turkeys among the rural residential properties along the road. Watch for them as you approach the parking area.

A few yards down the road from the parking area is a marshy slough on the right, where the creek is close by. Check here for watercentric species like red-winged blackbird, common yellowthroat, fox sparrow, and an occasional duck. On the left are the cliffs that hug the road for the first quarter mile. There is almost always a canyon wren somewhere on the cliffs; listen for its cascading song. Cordilleran flycatcher nests here. In this area and all along the road, deciduous trees and fruiting bushes attract such species as cedar waxwing, warbling vireo, both

Cliffs above brushy hillside

chickadees, blue jay, American robin, Bullock's oriole, white-breasted nuthatch, and migrating warblers.

A quarter mile down the road, the cliffs recede and the brushy slope below dominates the landscape. Here you will see a wide variety of birds that prefer this habitat, including both towhees, yellow-breasted chat, lazuli bunting, and American goldfinch. In the scattered pines among the brush, you may find black-headed grosbeak, red-breasted and pygmy nuthatches, Cassin's finch, lesser goldfinch, hairy woodpecker, and even Clark's nutcracker.

Cliffs to the north that have white-throated swifts

The corral

The new bridge that replaced the one destroyed in the 2013 flood

Ruby-crowned kinglet

As you proceed along the road, there are openings in the trees on the right side of the road that provide views of the higher cliffs across the highway. Scan these for common raven, golden eagle, and mixed flocks of white-breasted swifts and violet-green swallows. At 0.4 mile, you'll come upon barns and a small pasture, which can be good for Brewer's blackbird, barn swallow, and dark-eyed junco.

The remainder of the walk along the road should provide Townsend's solitaire, Lincoln's sparrow, and hermit thrush (in migration), chipping sparrow, and any species that can be found in the foothills.

At the turnaround point, a new bridge was constructed after the old bridge was destroyed in the flood of 2013. A quick visit to the bridge might yield an American dipper or a belted kingfisher. A party of birders could leave a car here for a ride back to the beginning of the hike, or, what the heck, just retrace your steps back along the road and see what other goodies you might have missed on the walk out.

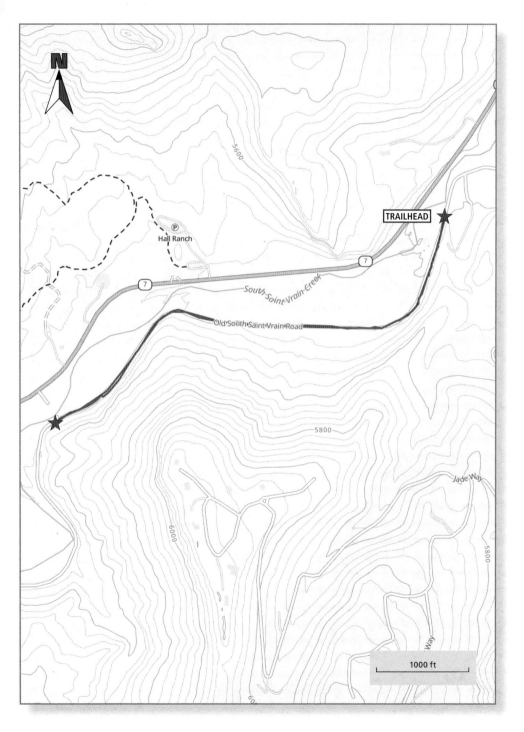

OLD SOUTH ST. VRAIN ROAD

Chapter 4. **Heil Valley Ranch**

ROUND-TRIP DISTANCE	3.85 miles
ELEVATION GAIN	417 feet
MAX ELEVATION	5,937 feet
TRAIL TYPE	Loop
DIFFICULTY	Easy
BEST SEASON(S)	Summer

FEATURED BIRDS: Wild turkey; American and lesser goldfinches; ruby-crowned and golden-crowned kinglets; mountain and black-capped chickadees; Steller's and blue jays; American crow/American raven; hairy and downy woodpeckers; red-naped sapsucker; northern flicker; American three-toed woodpecker; Cordilleran flycatchers; Hammond's, dusky, and western wood-pewee; all three nuthatches; Townsend's solitaire; spotted and green-tailed towhees; plumbeous vireo; western tanager; lazuli bunting; Macgillivray's and Virginia's warblers; siskin and house finch; red crossbill; and pine grosbeak
Special Bonus: northern pygmy-owl, common poorwill, or dusky grouse

COMMENT: Heil Valley Ranch is a Boulder County Open Space Park. At this writing there is no fee for admission or parking, but this could change in the future. Several of the more popular Boulder parks have fee parking.

Hiking the Overland Trail

The old Altona Schoolhouse

The park encompasses the former ranch and consists of open ponderosa forest with a few other tracts of habitat, including riparian thickets and brushy hillside. The park abuts the burn area of the Overland Fire of 2003, which created a large expanse of prairie on the adjoining ridge. There is historic interest here as well, as the area was settled by European colonists in the late 1800s. Altona had a schoolhouse, which has been preserved and can be seen on our hike. There are also salvaged railroad cars that once served as residences and outbuildings for the Heil Ranch.

As with many park-oriented hikes, there are a number of options at Heil Valley Ranch. The Lichen Loop, Wapiti, and Picture Rock Trails are also good for birding. If you have a bit of time and energy left after doing the Overland Trail, the Lichen Loop makes an excellent add-on (see page 40).

GETTING THERE: From the north (CO Highway 66) or south (Boulder), take Highway 36 to Lefthand Canyon Drive. The turnoff is about six miles south of the intersection with Highway 66—look for the Greenbriar Inn. Take Lefthand Canyon Drive 0.6 mile to the entrance to Heil Valley Ranch Park at Geer Road. Go north on Geer Road for 1.1 miles to the Main Trailhead parking lot.

The border of the Overland Fire

THE ROUTE: Our hike begins at the Main Trailhead parking lot. Check this area before setting off, as the moist thickets among the pines can have gray catbird and the pines may yield nuthatches or woodpeckers. Once you have had a look around, cross Geer Canyon Drive about two hundred yards to the south and pick up the Overland Loop trail. The trail makes a short climb to the left to an intersection; take the route to the left. From here, our route will follow an elongated figure-eight shape.

Hiking through a sumac-covered draw

The trail begins a long descent through open Ponderosa woodland. Along this one-mile stretch, the typical foothills pine forest specialists may appear. Watch and listen for white-breasted nuthatch, pine siskin, hairy woodpecker, and brown creeper. As the trail flattens and leaves the pines, you will come to a three-way intersection. This is the crossing point of the figure eight. Pass the first trail on the right and take the second, which puts you on the Schoolhouse Loop. Follow the trail along the log fenceline until you arrive at a small grove of pines and junipers. Check here for Townsend's solitaire, American robin, and perhaps Swainson's thrush in migration.

The trail soon takes a sharp left and crosses an open area of grassland. This is a fine place to find a flock of wild turkeys, who seem to divide their time between the grassy areas on the left and the irrigation ditch on the right.

At 0.7 mile from the Overland/ Schoolhouse junction, a short spur will take you to the old Altona Schoolhouse. There is information about the history of the schoolhouse

Williamson's sapsucker

and the surrounding patches of brush can be good for dark-eyed junco, white-crowned sparrow (especially in fall migration), and both goldfinches.

Return to the main trail, taking a few minutes to check the area around the canal. This riparian area can be surprising with gray catbird, chickadees, flycatchers, and towhees. Wild turkeys also frequent this area and along the canal.

Another quarter mile closes the Schoolhouse Loop. Along the way, you will pass the old corrals and a couple of boxcars that were once used as housing and storage space. There is information at a small kiosk. While this area doesn't tend to be birdy, it is worth checking the structures for possible nesting Say's phoebes and barn swallows.

Red crossbill

Chipping sparrow, a common nesting bird of the foothills ponderosa forests

You will return to the intersection from where you joined the Schoolhouse Loop earlier. Pass that point and take the next left turn a few yards up the trail. This is the Overland Loop, starting on the leg that runs a little higher up the ridge and adjacent to the Overland burn area. Watch along these open areas for mountain bluebirds and tree swallows in late spring/early summer. For the final mile and a half, the habitat along the trail is consistent, with open ponderosa forest bound by hillside prairie from the old burn. There are several small moist drainages that intersect the trail where you can see both towhees, dark-eyed junco, and any number of migrants that might take advantage of the ground cover. The pines are teeming with pygmy, white-, and red-breasted nuthatches. Mountain and black-capped chickadees, ruby-crowned (and with a little luck, golden-crowned) kinglets, Steller's and blue jays, Cassin's and house finches, and other typical species of the lower foothills are all possible.

The trail makes a modest descent back to the shelter, from where you can add the Lichen Loop if you are in the mood for a little extra distance and a few more birds.

NOTE: In October of 2020 the park was heavily damaged by the Calwood Fire. Most access to the park is closed until restoration can be completed. Check the park's website for current status.

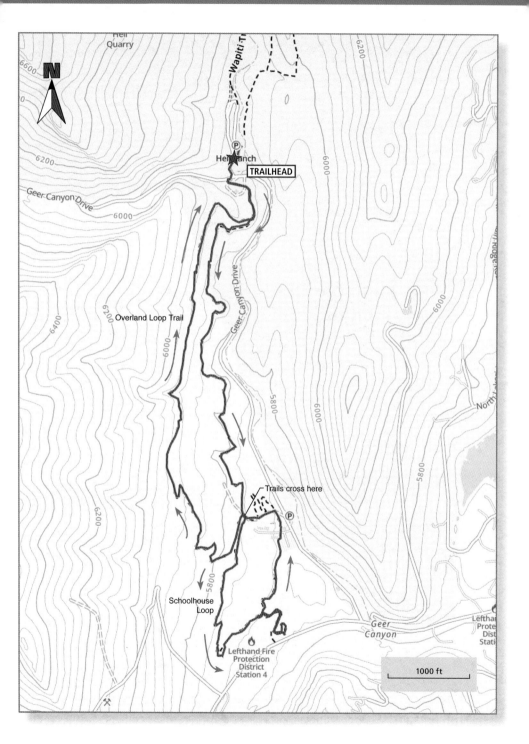

HEIL VALLEY RANCH

Chapter 5. The Lichen Loop

ROUND-TRIP DISTANCE	1.5 miles
ELEVATION GAIN	306 feet
MAX ELEVATION	6,139 feet
TRAIL TYPE	Loop
DIFFICULTY	Easy
BEST SEASON(S)	Summer

FEATURED BIRDS: See Heil Valley Ranch (page 34)

COMMENT: The Lichen is a short loop that tracks to the north from the same beginning point as the Heil Valley Ranch Overland Loop (see page 34). The birds and habitats are identical to those of Heil Valley Ranch, with a few minor differences and additional historical value. The trail is named appropriately; watch for a variety of lichens (a symbiotic combination of an algae and a fungus) on the rocks along the route.

THE ROUTE: This trail is simple. Begin at the shelter, cross the wooden foot bridge, and head north. Watch for wild turkeys, as they are frequently seen around the parking lot. In 0.2 mile, you will reach a junction. Go right and begin the gradual ascent up the valley. The trail makes a bend to the east and then returns to its northward trend. You will pass among large boulders that have come down from the ridge of Dakota Sandstone (representing the latest Cretaceous, the end of the Age of Dinosaurs) above on the right. The open meadow in the middle of the valley may have some of the same meadow-dwelling species like bluebirds, and the pines again may abound with pygmy nuthatches, mountain and black-capped chickadees, and Steller's jays.

The 0.7-mile mark is the high point of the trail; at 0.9 mile there is a junction that can be taken to connect with the Wapiti

Female red crossbill feeds in a Douglas fir

The cliffs overlooking the forest

and other trails to the north end of the park. At 1.2 miles, there is a short spur that leads to a kiln dating to settlement days. This kiln was not used for pottery but for the manufacture of charcoal and other useful materials.

Shortly thereafter is the junction that completes the loop and leaves a short stroll back to the parking lot.

The lichen for which the trail is named

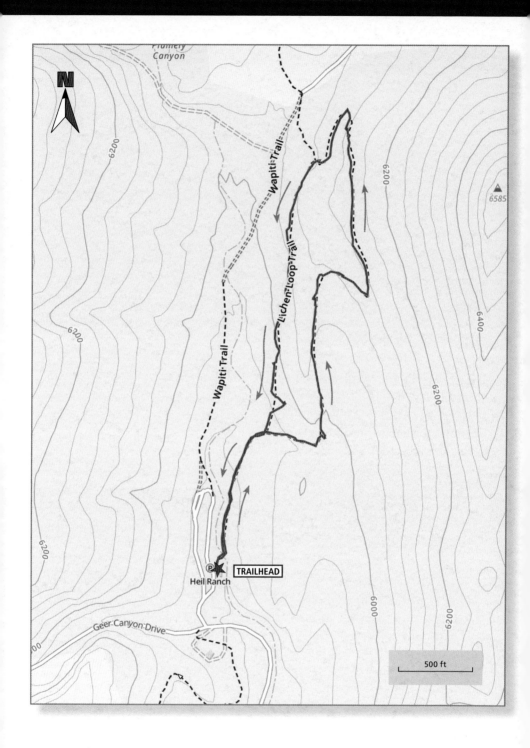

THE LICHEN LOOP

Chapter 6. Ouzel Falls

ROUND-TRIP DISTANCE	5.5 miles
ELEVATION GAIN	1,406 feet
MAX ELEVATION	9,452 feet
TRAIL TYPE	Out-and-back
DIFFICULTY	Moderate
BEST SEASON(S)	Summer

FEATURED BIRDS: Black swift; American dipper; ruby-crowned and golden-crowned kinglets; American three-toed woodpecker; red-breasted, white-breasted, and pygmy nuthatches; olive-sided flycatcher; dusky grouse; winter/Pacific wren; and most typical coniferous forest mountain birds

COMMENT: The Ouzel Falls hike is in the Wild Basin area of Rocky Mountain National Park. This is a fee area. While this trail is similar to other foothills trails, it is included because of the potential presence of one hard-to-find species: black

Ouzel Falls *(photo by Frank Burzynski)*

Brown creeper

swift. These mysterious birds nest behind or near waterfalls and most known nesting locations are in remote areas with difficult access. Along with Box Canyon in Ouray, Ouzel Falls is a rare opportunity to see this species without difficulty.

"Water ouzel" is the historic name for American dipper, a bird that is wedded closely to foothills stream habitat. This little bird has the thickest feather density of any bird. It is as at home walking on the bottom of a stream as it is perching on a rock. The dipper will not be seen away from a stream. Watch for midstream rocks with whitewash on them to locate customary perches of this bird.

GETTING THERE: The Ouzel Falls hike can be reached via CO Highway 7, from either Estes Park to the north or Allenspark to the south. Look for the turnoff to the Wild Basin section of Rocky Mountain National Park. From the entrance station, follow the road west about two miles to the Wild Basin Trailhead.

THE ROUTE: The Ouzel Falls hike is an up-and-back route, following North St. Vrain Creek for most of the trail's length; the falls are situated on Ouzel Creek. Our

American dipper

hike begins at the Wild Basin Ranger Station parking lot. Birding around the lot can be good, so take a few minutes to check the moist thickets for Wilson's and MacGillivray's warblers and Lincoln's sparrow before starting up the trail.

Shortly after leaving the trailhead you will come to a series of rapids called Copeland Falls. From here, the trail winds through mixed coniferous forest, which hosts a suite of typical mountain birds, including hairy woodpecker, red-naped and Williamson's sapsucker, mountain chickadee, all three nuthatches, olive-sided flycatcher, ruby-crowned and golden-crowned kinglets, Cassin's finch, and evening grosbeak.

About a mile and a quarter past Copeland Falls is a trail junction. The right fork follows North St. Vrain Creek toward Thunder Lake; our route follows the left fork and soon crosses a footbridge over the creek. This is a good spot to watch and listen for American dipper. The dipper is rather drab, entirely dark gray (note, however, the flashes of the white nictitating membrane when the bird blinks), but makes up for it in behavior and song. The song is high-pitched whistles and trills. It is lovely, but the most distinctive feature of this bird is its knee bends. It will bob several times like an athlete and then jump into the rushing water, oblivious to the cold, and walk on the bottom of the stream in search of invertebrates. The dipper is migratory, only in that it will move to lower elevations in winter, so it is present in foothills and montane streams year-round. In the winter, watch the bird leap into holes in the ice and emerge a few seconds later like a cork popping from a bottle.

After spending a little time at the bridge, a quick side trip to see the Calypso Cascades can be worthwhile, then continue along the trail to the west. In a little less

Ouzel Falls *(photo by Frank Burzynski)*

than a mile you will reach Ouzel Creek. Take the short side spur to the left to reach the base of Ouzel Falls.

At this writing, there is at least one active black swift nest at the falls. Nests can be difficult to spot, so scan the rock walls around the falls carefully. The nest will appear to be not much more than a dark blob in a crevice or on a ledge. The swifts tend to be crepuscular, so optimal times to see activity are dawn and dusk.

Our birding route ends at Ouzel Falls. Those who wish to add additional miles (and scenery) can continue for a couple of miles up the trail to Ouzel Lake, or two miles beyond that to Bluebird Lake. Follow the trail back to the parking lot. Along the way, check the tops of trees for olive-sided flycatcher and listen for its "Quick! Three beers!" song. In years of good cone crops, you may find red crossbill, and with a little luck, a flock of colorful evening grosbeaks.

Bighorn sheep *(photo by Frank Burzynski)*

OUZEL FALLS

Chapter 7

Ptarmigan Ptrio

One of the most sought-after birds in Colorado is the white-tailed ptarmigan. These elusive birds dwell at or above treeline, which in Colorado is found at approximately 11,000 feet elevation. This makes accessing areas where they can be found a challenge. Few roads are at this elevation, and hikes to reach the proper habitat tend to be long and strenuous. The birds can be found on the flanks of almost any 13er or 14er, but unless you are in excellent condition and accustomed to high-elevation hiking, these trails can be arduous, to say the least.

Our ptarmigan hikes begin and end above treeline, feature spectacular scenery, and can be accessed by a main road. "Ptarmigan Ptrio" includes one site in Rocky Mountain National Park, one on the flanks of Mounts Evans and Bierstadt, and one that traverses a glacial cirque above Loveland Pass.

This chapter includes three sites that are known to host ptarmigan. Do not, however, assume that just by visiting the sites you will be assured of seeing them. Even in excellent habitat, seeing these birds presents several challenges. First, although the hikes are short and easy, they are above 11,000 feet, which calls for a certain amount of caution. In addition, ptarmigan have plumage superbly adapted to the conditions in their preferred habitat; they are tundra-colored in the summer and white in winter, which makes them almost invisible against seasonal backgrounds. One can almost step on the birds and not see them. Watching for movement is the best way to pick them out. In spring and fall, partial molt can leave them more visible as they transition from their white phase and back. In any case, you will have the privilege of looking for special birds, so put on your high-elevation hiking hat and enjoy!

Part A. **Guanella Pass**

ROUND-TRIP DISTANCE	2.5 miles
ELEVATION GAIN	535 feet
MAX ELEVATION	12,005 feet
TRAIL TYPE	Loop
DIFFICULTY	Easy to moderate
BEST SEASON(S)	Summer and winter

FEATURED BIRDS: White-tailed ptarmigan, American pipit, mountain white-crowned sparrow, fox sparrow, and Wilson's warbler

COMMENT: Part of the Ptarmigan Ptrio, Guanella Pass is intermediate in difficulty between the other two hikes in the trio, Medicine Bow Curve and Loveland Pass. There are multiple routes that one can take to survey the area for ptarmigan, but the one suggested here was chosen to include enough distance and elevation gain to create a hike. For the more ambitious, Guanella Pass is also the trailhead for the Mount Bierstadt Trail, a popular 14er.

Above treeline, the area is characterized by typical alpine tundra and willow thickets, which define the rather limited avifauna found there.

Fox sparrow

Guanella Pass Road

NOTE: Best Season above has included winter; this needs some qualification. In the past, the county has plowed Guanella Pass Road, providing easy access to the area described here. As a result, Guanella Pass was arguably the best site in Colorado to see ptarmigan in their white winter plumage. The area was popular among birders as a snowshoe destination.

Unfortunately, at the time of this writing the road is no longer being plowed, making the pass virtually inaccessible in winter. However, it is worth checking to see if plowing might be resumed at some future time and the area restored to its former glory as a winter ptarmigan superstar location.

The willow thickets that host songbirds and sustain ptarmigan in winter

GETTING THERE: Take I-70 west from Denver for about forty-five miles to Exit 228 at Georgetown. It is 11.5 miles from the exit to the pass. To get there, go west (right) at the roundabout, merging onto Argentine Street. Argentine will become Brownell Street in about a half mile, when it enters the downtown area. At the T, turn left onto 6th Street, go two blocks

The "Sawtooth" between Mounts Bierstadt and Evans

to Rose Street, and turn right. Proceed four blocks on Rose to Guanella Pass Road and follow it to the pass.

THE ROUTE: The Guanella Pass hike might be better described as a wander; the ultimate destination for the hike is an unnamed high point about a mile south of the pass. There is a well-established trail that goes south from the parking area but quickly deteriorates into a web of poorly defined tracks. The route illustrated here follows the trail, then available access points through the dense thickets. These willows are a food source for the ptarmigan in winter and provide shelter in summer. As you walk the area, be alert for ptarmigan that have strayed from the willows and are out in the open.

There are several other birds of interest that can be found in the area. As in other similar areas, dark-lored "mountain" white-crowned sparrows nest near treeline, and American pipit is ubiquitous on the tundra. In addition, the thickets host nesting Wilson's warbler and fox sparrow. Listen for the sweet song of the Wilson's and the more complex song of the fox sparrow as they sing from perches on the willows.

To complete the suggested route, circle around to the south side of the high point, where there is more open terrain to enhance ptarmigan potential. Summit the point and enjoy the views of Mounts Evans and Bierstadt. Return to the parking lot via any route that looks attractive.

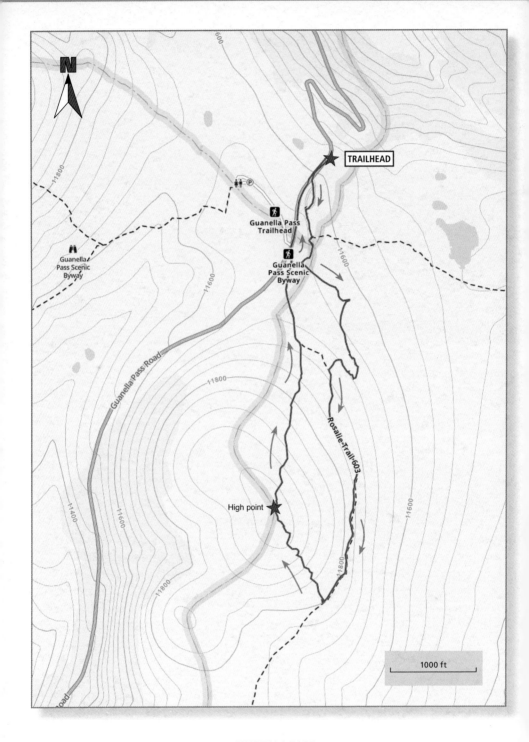

GUANELLA PASS

Part B. Loveland Pass

ROUND-TRIP DISTANCE	3.25 miles
ELEVATION GAIN	969 feet
MAX ELEVATION	12,480 feet
TRAIL TYPE	Loop
DIFFICULTY	Moderate
BEST SEASON(S)	Summer

FEATURED BIRDS: White-tailed ptarmigan, American pipit, and "mountain" white-crowned sparrow

COMMENT: Loveland Pass is the most difficult trail of the trio, as it is longer and has more elevation gain than the other two. However, the difficulty lies not in length or elevation gain, but that the trail begins at almost 12,000 feet and goes up from there. This trail combines an opportunity to see ptarmigan with world-class scenery. The route follows ridges above a cirque, which is a basin carved by ice accumulation and movement at the head of an ancient alpine glacier. Views from the ridges are spectacular in all directions. There is a small cirque lake at the uppermost end of the cirque that can have a marvelous display of wildflowers.

White-tailed ptarmigan in summer plumage

American pipit nests on the "tundra" here

GETTING THERE: Take I-70 west from Denver for approximately sixty miles. Take Exit 216 to Highway 6. This is the last exit before the Johnson-Eisenhower Tunnel, and is also the exit for the Loveland Basin and Arapahoe Basin Ski Areas. Follow Highway 6 for approximately four miles to the pass.

THE ROUTE: Begin at the parking lot of the pass and take the trail that heads southwest, following the ridge and a small adjacent rocky swale on your left. Look for ptarmigan along the lower section of the trail, as the birds are frequently seen in the boulder field in this small drainage. The trail rises steadily for three-quarters of a mile as you climb toward the top of the ridge, and the birds can be anywhere along here. You will soon reach a saddle in the ridge that provides great views to the south. Here the trail turns west and continues following the ridge for another three-quarters of a mile to an unnamed high point with an elevation of 12,479 feet. This is the end point of our route. From here you can backtrack if you wish. However, another option with additional

Pika—denizen of the boulder fields

birding potential begins by retracing your steps for about a quarter mile and watching for an area where the slope down to the base of the ridge is moderate. There is no established trail here, but you can easily bushwhack your way down the hill, taking a route that will bring you to the small cirque lake at the bottom. It is in this area that wildflowers are most abundant.

From the lake, walk east for a couple hundred yards until you come to a small creek. Follow this creek downslope for a half mile, where it crosses another trail. As you walk along the creek, watch for American pipits and listen for their flight calls. Follow this path to the east to return to the parking lot. However, do not be in a hurry here, as along the lower part of this trail conifers and bushes begin to appear. This is where the white-crowned sparrows nest. Watch for them perched on the tops of small trees.

The boulder fields along the trail are home to one of the iconic mammals of the mountain west, the pika. This small member of the rabbit family inhabits dens among the huge rocks. With a little luck, you may see one scampering about with a mouthful of grass, headed to its den to make preparations for winter hibernation.

Lower trail from the rim of the cirque

LOVELAND PASS

Part C. Rocky Mountain National Park, Medicine Bow Curve

ROUND-TRIP DISTANCE	1 mile
ELEVATION GAIN	306 feet
MAX ELEVATION	11,727 feet
TRAIL TYPE	Out-and-back
DIFFICULTY	Easy
BEST SEASON(S)	Summer

FEATURED BIRDS: White-tailed ptarmigan, "mountain" white-crowned sparrow, American pipit, and brown-capped rosy-finch

COMMENT: Medicine Bow Curve is in Rocky Mountain National Park, and as such is a fee area. The hike is quite easy except that it is entirely above 11,000 feet, where even a short stroll can leave a hiker short of breath. Pack and prepare accordingly for all weather, and watch for signs of altitude illness. Please remain on the well-worn trail; as the slogan goes, "Alpine vegetation grows by the inch and dies by the foot."

GETTING THERE: In Rocky Mountain National Park, Medicine Bow Curve can be found 0.5 mile west of the Alpine Visitor Center on Trail Ridge Road.

Trail across the "tundra" with the Mummy Range in the distance

Rocky terrain along the trail, favored by ptarmigan

THE ROUTE: Medicine Bow Curve is the easiest of the Ptarmigan Ptrio hikes. Park at the curve and take the obvious trail north across the tundra (it is not actually tundra, which is permanently frozen ground, but since it is popularly known as such, who are we to argue). Ptarmigan can be seen anywhere along the trail; I have seen them wandering in the parking lot. However, sightings here are sporadic and the birds are best detected by movement. This route follows the established trail to the north until it gradually disappears as the flat pediment begins to drop to the valley below.

Other birds of interest along the trail are the black-lored "mountain" white-crowned sparrow and American pipit. Check for the sparrows around the scattered krummholz ("twisted wood" in German, dwarf conifers found around treeline), where they nest. Over the open rocky tundra, listen for the calls of displaying pipits. These high-elevation nesters make impressive mating flights, and when they land, their buffy coloration blends perfectly with the terrain.

Alpine forget-me-not, one of the dwarf wildflowers found above treeline

Other than a few American robins (demonstrating habitat adaptability) and common ravens, there is only one other regularly occurring species of interest here: the elusive and highly sought-after brown-capped rosy-finch. The finches nest at nearby Lava Cliffs, but prefer the food that can be gleaned from snowfields. There is one such large snow patch at the end of this trail, and the finches occasionally can be seen wandering around it.

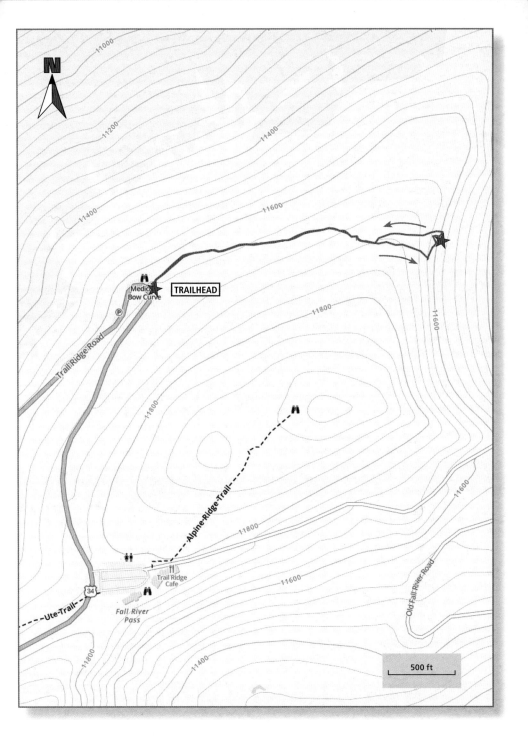

ROCKY MOUNTAIN NATIONAL PARK, MEDICINE BOW CURVE

Chapter 8. **Mesa Complex/Doudy Draw**

ROUND-TRIP DISTANCE	5 miles
ELEVATION GAIN	943 feet
MAX ELEVATION	6,421 feet
TRAIL TYPE	Loop (Mesa); out-and-back (Doudy Draw)
DIFFICULTY	Moderate
BEST SEASON(S)	Summer

FEATURED BIRDS: Yellow-breasted chat; gray catbird; Bullock's oriole; lazuli bunting; warbling vireo; western meadowlark; yellow, Virginia's, and Macgillivray's warblers; lesser goldfinch; black-headed grosbeak; brown creeper; pine siskin; western tanager; ovenbird; all three nuthatches; hairy woodpecker; and red-naped sapsucker

COMMENT: The Mesa Trail complex includes a variety of trails. Our route will include several of them, but there are many options for other desirable routes. This is a fee area unless you are a Boulder County resident. This complex of trails is part

Blue grosbeak

Mountain bluebird

Bullock's oriole   Yellow-breasted chat

of the Boulder trail network and connects to other trails, creating a variety of hiking/birding options outside of the route described here. The setting for these trails is dramatic, as they are situated at the base of the spectacular Flatirons formations. There are restrooms at the parking lot and 0.3 mile down the Doudy Draw Trail.

GETTING THERE: Go north from Golden, or south from Boulder, on CO Highway 93 to Eldorado Springs Drive (CO Highway 170). Go west for 1.6 miles and turn right into the parking lot access.

THE ROUTE: We begin at the parking lot and walk north, cross the bridge over South Boulder Creek, and pass the stone homestead house. It should be noted that if you wish to add a few more birds to your list, either before starting or at the end of the hike, you can turn left as you leave the parking lot and follow the creek to the west. Among the trees along the creek are western wood-pewee, warbling vireo, and several swallow species. Cedar waxwings can sometimes be seen flycatching over the creek. However, this detour is not included in our hike, so continue following the Mesa Trail (which appears at several different locations) about a quarter mile until it intersects with the Homestead Trail. Turn left (west) onto the Homestead Trail. There is a gradual ascent across prairies with numerous clumps of sumac, wild plum, and other low-growing, brushy plants which host Virginia's warbler and, in the wetter areas, MacGillivray's warbler. Western meadowlarks provide background music.

About a half mile up the Homestead Trail, ponderosa pines begin to appear, at first scattered and then in greater numbers as elevation increases. Begin to

Plumbeous vireo

listen for the raspy question-and-answer song of plumbeous vireo, the robin-with-a-sore-throat song of western tanager, several species of woodpeckers and nuthatches, and brown creeper. Ovenbirds nest in these areas. A little over a mile up the Homestead Trail, it again meets the Mesa Trail, and our route follows the Mesa Trail for another mile. Anywhere along these upper sections of trail you might encounter dusky, Hammond's, or olive-sided flycatchers. There are also junctions with the Shadow Canyon Trails, which provide access to additional habitats in Shadow Canyon to the west.

Throughout this section of the Mesa Trail, the route is in ponderosa forest with a few stream crossings. Check these areas for yellow-breasted chat and MacGillivray's warbler. As the trail continues to wind up the sides of shallow valleys, it passes through a number of areas of more open woodland. These sites provide excellent views of the drainages below and the riparian and mountain meadow habitats adjoining them. Pause here and watch for a bit. Birds of many species can be seen flying across these open areas, perching in the surrounding forest margins, or working the areas around the little streams. Watch especially for lesser goldfinch, yellow-breasted chat, or gray catbird.

White-breasted nuthatch

After a mile of gradual climbing, the Mesa Trail meets the Upper Big Bluestem Trail. This is the route we follow for our descent. Follow Upper Big Bluestem for a little over a mile, past three switchbacks to its intersection with Lower Big Bluestem, which drops to a junction with the Mesa Trail (again!). Go left on the Mesa Trail, which loops around and returns to the trailhead.

If you would like to add a bit more length and habitat you can go right on the Mesa Trail and follow it to the Towhee Trail. The Towhee eventually reconnects to the Mesa Trail. The descent passes through the habitats we visited on the way up, but of course in reverse order.

Bonus: **Doudy Draw Extension**

ROUND-TRIP DISTANCE	0.7 mile
DIFFICULTY	Easy
ELEVATION GAIN	Minimal

COMMENT: To add a little distance, and more importantly, birds, take the Doudy Draw Trail after finishing the Mesa complex. The trailhead/parking lot for Doudy is directly across the road from the Mesa parking lot. See map on page 64.

THE ROUTE: From the parking area, follow the trail south. The interesting part of the trail ends at the Community Ditch, in about a third of a mile. The birds along this stretch are the same as the prairie portions of the Mesa Trail, with a couple of additions. In migration, sage thrasher is frequently found, especially around the parking area. As you walk south, take note of the thicket on the right (west) side of the trail. This little patch appeals to yellow-breasted chat and Bullock's oriole. A bit farther along are some brushy areas on the east side. Check this area for blue-gray gnatcatcher, lesser goldfinch, and especially blue grosbeak, which has been known to nest here. At the end of this stretch of trail is a cottonwood grove adjacent to the ditch, which can have some of the same species as found along South Boulder Creek.

Sage thrasher

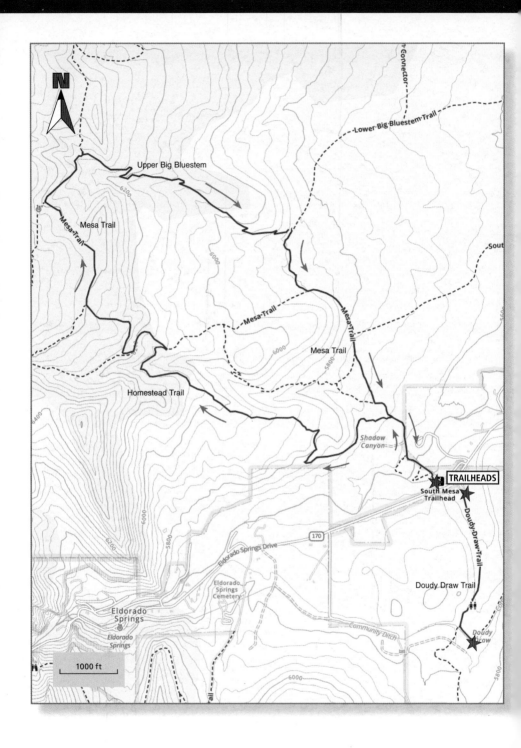

MESA COMPLEX/DOUDY DRAW

Chapter 9: **Barr Lake State Park**

ROUND-TRIP DISTANCE	9.7 miles
ELEVATION GAIN	Minimal
MAX ELEVATION	5,110 feet
TRAIL TYPE	Loop
DIFFICULTY	Moderate
BEST SEASON(S)	Spring and fall

FEATURED BIRDS: Ducks, grebes, loons, American white pelican, double-crested cormorant, shorebirds, songbirds, and numerous species of gulls

COMMENT: Barr Lake State Park is one of the outstanding birding sites in Colorado and has been recognized by the American Bird Conservancy as an Important Bird Area. The Bird Conservancy of the Rockies (BCOR) has its headquarters at the Stone House by the dam. Birding at the park is good in all seasons, with optimum times being spring and fall, when migrant songbirds are joined by throngs of waterfowl. Barr Lake is also a nesting site for bald eagles.

The geographic setting of the park includes the lake (the water is owned by agricultural interests, not the state), a sizable tract of land featuring a variety of habitats, and the Burlington Ditch, which parallels the lake on its south side. It should be noted that in years with less rainfall, water is drawn from the reservoir for agricultural use, which can expose large tracts of mudflats. This in turn attracts a wide variety of shorebirds in fall migration.

Also, during fall migration, BCOR operates a banding station, which provides an additional opportunity to see birds in the hand. The banding station is located a quarter mile east of the visitor center; our hike includes a potential stop there if you wish to include it, in season.

GETTING THERE: From Denver, take I-76 toward Brighton and exit at Bromley Lane. Turn right and follow Bromley for about three-quarters of a mile. Turn right (south) on Picadilly Road and follow it about a mile and a half to the park entrance. Follow the signs to the visitor center.

THE ROUTE: Our hike begins near the visitor center, at the footbridge across the ditch. It is a loop and can be walked either way; for purposes of this book, it is taken clockwise. From the bridge, turn left and immediately bear right from the service

American goldfinch

road and onto the Neidrach Trail. This spur off the road (which doubles as the trail for much of its route) passes near to the lake shore, with great viewing of waterfowl and shorebirds in season, then continues to a boardwalk and viewing kiosk.

The area near the lake, prior to reaching the boardwalk, has views and/or access to the lakeshore and large expanses of exposed lake bottom in the fall. As the reservoir is drawn down for agricultural use, vast areas of mudflat may be created and a variety of shorebirds may be seen here, including black-necked stilt, American avocet, black-bellied (and, with a little luck, American golden) plover, stilt sandpiper, sanderling, pectoral sandpiper, and most of the peeps. You can leave the trail and walk toward the shoreline of the lake (wherever that may be, depending upon water level) for excellent, unobstructed views of the lake and shore. There may be hundreds of American white pelicans, double-crested cormorants, or western grebes along with smaller (but still large!) numbers of geese, ducks, coots, and grebes.

Some of the thousands of American white pelicans that assemble at the lake

Boardwalk and viewing platform along the Neidrach Trail

Return to the trail and proceed along the boardwalk. The trees surrounded by water on the left (south) side of the boardwalk often host warblers and other songbirds in migration. The kiosk offers views of the west end of the lake, and also of two notable features of Barr Lake on the opposite side of the reservoir: the bald eagle nest (which has been used by eagles for many years) and a huge double-crested cormorant colony, utilized by hundreds of pairs of cormorants. There are also terrific binocular views of Longs Peak in Rocky Mountain National Park. At the end of the boardwalk, the trail rejoins the maintenance road. The prairies to the left (south) side of the trail have western meadowlark singing from the tops of mullein, ringnecked pheasants darting among the brush, and barn swallows cruising for flying insects. Check for western and eastern kingbirds along the fence lines.

From the visitor center, it is about 1.5 miles to the trail spur that accesses the boardwalk and gazebo. The gazebo provides additional excellent viewing of the eagle nest and cormorant colony as well as the flotillas of waterfowl that cover the lake in spring and fall. Large numbers of Canada and cackling geese can be seen here (in winter, when the lake is still not frozen), as well as smaller numbers of snow and Ross's geese. Check the vegetation along the boardwalk for songbirds in migration. Many Bullock's orioles nest here, and western wood-pewees are common.

Footbridge at the beginning of the hike

As you round the southwest end of the lake, the habitat along the shore includes more marsh and wet woodland. Flycatchers find this to their liking. Eastern and western kingbirds, Say's phoebe, and occasionally willow flycatcher can be seen here. Watch the shaded, more secluded areas for blue-winged and cinnamon teal, as well as wood duck.

Just after you cross the inlet canal there is a short spur trail leading off to the right. A walk down this short trail can be worthwhile, as it follows the canal. The surrounding greenery may have numerous species. Check the moist shrubby areas for gray catbird and yellow warbler.

Blue grosbeak and lazuli bunting may be found anywhere along this stretch of trail in the open areas. In summer, you should see many flyovers of cormorants and great blue herons that share the nesting area. Swainson's and red-tailed hawks also cruise the perimeter in search of the small mammals and snakes that make up much of their diet.

From this point, the habitat is the same as found along most of the lake, with mixed cottonwoods, marshes, and arid prairie. Keep checking the woodlands for the abundant western wood-pewees and the thickets of thistle and other seed-bearing plants for American goldfinches and pine siskins in season.

You will not find a great deal of variety until you reach the abrupt bend in the trail to the east, at about the 6.3-mile mark. Our route continues across the dam, from which you can see vast numbers of waterfowl in spring and fall, and in winter when the lake is not frozen. Many species of gulls can be seen here, too. In addition to throngs of ring-billed, numbers of herring (winter), California (summer) and Franklin's (migration) gulls, many other gull species have been recorded here including Sabine's (rare but regular in migration), mew, Iceland, lesser black-backed (fairly numerous in winter), glaucous, and great black-backed.

A couple of additional miles and species can be added by detouring from this route at the beginning (north end) of the dam and taking the road below that passes by the Bird Conservatory of the Rockies (BCOR) headquarters at the Stone House and drops to the fields and marshes beyond. Here there is a drainage ditch that parallels the dam. In the marshes along the ditch, Virginia's rail and sora are sometimes found, and winter wren is seen frequently in winter in dense thickets. Northern harriers course above the marshes, and red-tailed hawks nest in the cottonwoods.

Return to our main route, after crossing the dam, where the trail follows the shoreline around to the boat launch area, another fine spot for viewing the lake. A half mile farther is a short spur that follows a boardwalk out to a viewing blind that is worth a look. The marshes along the boardwalk can have rails and marsh wren. Return to the trail and continue along the canal. The trail passes through much riparian vegetation that is good for many of the species we have seen previously, as well as sparrows along the brushy banks. In winter, white-crowned sparrows are abundant and Harris's sparrow is sometimes seen with them. Northern

Barr Lake State Park visitor center

Female northern harrier

flicker and downy woodpecker are year-round residents. Look for the nesting platform that almost always hosts a family of osprey in summer.

Another point of interest is the BCOR banding station, which is a must-see in the fall. The banders here welcome visitors and willingly share their captures along with great information as to the birds they are banding. The nest box near the banding station often has a nesting barn owl, and the woodlands and nearby willow thicket are a great place to find warblers, vireos, chickadees, and flycatchers. Listen for the rapid up-and-down song of the warbling vireo.

A few hundred yards down the trail is the bridge back to the visitor center area (where the bird feeders are worth a look; a painted bunting appeared here several years ago), and we have completed the loop.

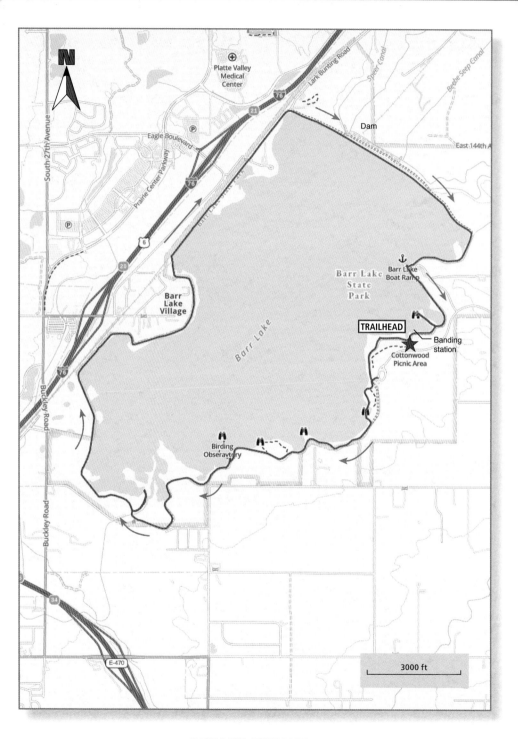

BARR LAKE STATE PARK

Chapter 10. Urban South Platte River

ROUND-TRIP DISTANCE	16 miles
ELEVATION GAIN	289 feet
MAX ELEVATION	5,125 feet
TRAIL TYPE	Out-and-back
DIFFICULTY	Moderate
BEST SEASON(S)	Winter

FEATURED BIRDS: Almost all diving and dabbling ducks that winter in Colorado, Barrow's goldeneye, pied-billed grebe, bald eagle, belted kingfisher, song and American tree sparrows, killdeer and Wilson's snipe (the only two shorebirds that winter in Colorado), great blue heron, black-crowned night-heron, gulls, northern harrier, and red-tailed hawk

COMMENT: The Urban South Platte River will never be confused with a garden spot, especially near the beginning of our hike. The area is highly industrialized, not to mention there is a large water treatment facility nearby that adds nothing to the general ambiance. However, none of these factors detract from the fact that this stretch of the South Platte has developed a reputation as being the best place in this part of Colorado to see waterfowl in winter. As ponds, lakes, and reservoirs freeze, ducks, geese, and other waterbirds are forced onto remaining open water, which generally means moving water, and the South Platte is the largest flowing waterway in the region. A good winter's day on the Platte can yield an astounding seventeen species of ducks without any rarities. Add geese, grebes, coots, and herons and the potential list of waterfowl alone can approach twenty-five.

Although waterfowl are the main attraction, there are plenty of other birds along the banks and in the riparian vegetation to make for an exciting day. Wilson's snipe, belted kingfisher, several sparrows, and a variety of raptors are regular here. American pipit may be present and rusty blackbirds occur occasionally.

Northern pintail and Barrow's goldeneye

A beneficial characteristic of this trail is that it has multiple access points. The south half of the trail, in addition to the starting point, may be accessed at Steele Street Park (78th Ave. at Steele St.) or at Platte River Trailhead Park (88th Ave. at Colorado Blvd.). The north part of the trail (north of 88th Ave.) can be accessed at Pelican Ponds Open space at Riverdale Road and 94th Avenue.

NOTE: There are no restrooms along this route.

GETTING THERE: Take I-25 to the 58th Avenue exit and go east to York Street. At York, go left (north) for a quarter mile to a nondescript parking lot on the right, adjacent to the river. There is a footbridge across the river just north of the parking lot.

NOTE: This hike is ideal for those wishing to do a little shorter or less time-consuming hike. There are many access points to the trail, with two of the most popular being at Steele Street Park at 78th Ave. and Steele Street, and the Platte River Trailhead Park at 88th Ave. and Colorado Blvd. Each has a spacious parking lot.

THE ROUTE: Our hike begins at the parking lot. There is a footbridge north of the lot and, although we will not cross it for purposes of this route, it is worth checking. Walk out and have a look up and down the river.

After leaving the footbridge, you will pass a section of the river with many gravel bars and lots of trees on the east bank. Check the gravel bars for pipits and snipe. The trees in this area are frequented by flocks of black-crowned night-herons, which, for whatever reason, are found here in greater numbers than elsewhere along the river. Look closely, as the coloration of these birds tends to make them invisible among the gray limbs of dead and leafless trees.

The "rapids" at the green storage tank

A typical stretch of the South Platte River

At the half-mile mark are effluent discharge channels and at the three-quarter-mile mark is the mouth of Sand Creek. The stretch of river in between is a favorite for ducks because of the nutrients from the inflow and action of the rough water that brings up materials from the riverbed. This is a good place for large numbers and variety of waterfowl. Non-waterfowl species that frequent the area include belted kingfisher, bushtit, song sparrow, American pipit, and white-crowned sparrow.

The habitat along the river and bird species remain much the same for the next two miles, as the trail passes under I-76 and 74th Avenue and reaches Steele Street Park. This is a popular access point for birders and offers views of the river and a wide variety of ducks.

Walking north from the park, at 3.3 miles you will be across the river from a large green storage tank. This tank is the landmark for one of the most favorable waterfowl viewing areas of the river, just above and below an artificial rapid. This is the best area to find Barrow's goldeneye in winter and is popular with many other diving ducks, including common goldeneye, lesser scaup, bufflehead, redhead, and mergansers. As you pass the green tank and the rapid, the Thornton Gravel Ponds are on the west side of the trail. If the ponds are not entirely frozen, they may have some interesting birds. Mergansers seem to favor these ponds.

Less than a mile downstream of the rapid is the Platte River Trailhead Park at 88th Avenue, just over 4 miles from our starting point. This is another popular starting and finishing point for birding groups. As such, we will reset our mileage here and proceed north, starting from zero miles at the Platte River Trailhead Park. The north portion of the trail has more woodland than the south and is therefore more favorable for songbirds in addition to waterfowl.

Three-quarters of a mile north of the starting point is a pond with a picnic shelter. This pond may have a few ducks but is unlikely to have any birds not found on the river. For a mile past the pond, however, the open space on the east side of the river expands and has open woodlands that may host a variety of songbirds. Look for nuthatches, house finch, American goldfinch, and red-winged blackbirds.

Once the trail clears the wooded areas, borrow pit ponds dominate the landscape. Over the years, there have been many operations that removed sand and gravel from the floodplain of the South Platte River. These pits have subsequently filled with water and form a series of sizable ponds and lakes. These bodies of water are large enough that they host not only diving and dabbling ducks, but periodically may have grebes, loons, and even scoters.

The first lake will be found at the 1.8-mile mark. Shortly thereafter, at 2.3 miles, the trail crosses McKay Road. Just past McKay Road is another lake. At 2.65 miles, the hiker will encounter an interesting site that provides views of the lake to the west (this area seems to attract lots of gulls) and a marsh on the east side of the trail. A short side trip along the marsh can be productive, as it hosts song and American tree sparrows, wintering Virginia rail, and perhaps a swamp sparrow.

Leaving the marsh, the trail turns north and passes yet another lake on the west. At 3.5 miles, the trail passes under 104th Avenue and enters Elaine T. Valente Open Space. The open space includes more ponds but also has some lightly wooded prairie, which has more wintering songbirds, including western meadowlark and Say's phoebe.

Adult (below) and juvenile (above) black-crowned night-herons

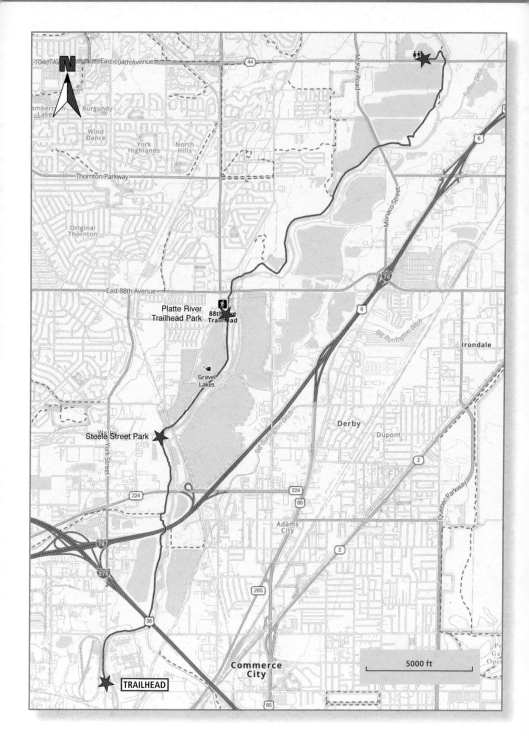

URBAN SOUTH PLATTE RIVER

Chapter 11. White Ranch Park

ROUND-TRIP DISTANCE	7.5 miles
ELEVATION GAIN	1,770 feet
MAX ELEVATION	7,485 feet
TRAIL TYPE	Loop
DIFFICULTY	Strenuous
BEST SEASON(S)	Spring and early summer

FEATURED BIRDS: Spotted and green-tailed towhees; black-headed grosbeak; lazuli bunting; broad-tailed hummingbird; yellow-breasted chat; western wood-pewee; yellow and Virginia's warblers; blue-gray gnatcatcher; warbling vireo; pygmy, white-breasted, and red-breasted nuthatches; pine siskin; dark-eyed junco (gray-headed race); hairy woodpecker; Steller's jay; Empidonax flycatchers; and red crossbill (all seasons, but dependent upon cone crop)

COMMENT: White Ranch Park is a Jefferson County Open Space park. There are restrooms at the lower (east) parking lot and the upper parking lot. Trails are wide and well maintained, but rocky in places. Sturdy hiking footwear is recommended. This hike is best undertaken on weekdays; the park is heavily used, especially on weekends, with a large population of mountain bikers.

Lazuli bunting

As with many of the parks, White Ranch Park has a complex of trails. The route described here is just one of many possibilities. It was chosen because it combines a fairly strenuous hike with a nice variety of birding opportunities. A hiker who wishes to add some additional difficulty could substitute the Mustang Trail (about halfway to the top) for the upper part of the Belcher Hill Trail/Sawmill Trail. Additional birding among the pines is possible by adding the Rawhide Trail, a four-mile loop beginning and ending at the upper parking lot. To do the Rawhide Trail only, the Upper White Ranch parking lot can be accessed by going west on Golden Gate Canyon Road, then going north on Crawford Gulch Road. Take Crawford Gulch to Belcher Hill Road and turn east (right) to the parking lot.

The trail enters the riparian woodland

GETTING THERE: From Golden, proceed north on CO Highway 93 for approximately one mile to the intersection of 93 and the well-signed 56th Avenue/White Ranch Park. Go west (left) and follow 56th Ave. for one mile to where it makes a T-intersection with Pine Ridge Road. Go north (right) on Pine Ridge a short distance to the east parking lot.

Spotted towhee

THE ROUTE: Our hike covers two areas known informally as Lower White Ranch and Upper White Ranch. The Belcher Hill Trail begins at the east parking lot (Lower White Ranch or east entrance) and goes north for several hundred yards (through private property). It passes through a gate and turns abruptly west. Some of the best birding along this route is found here for the next half mile. You will first pass through a mature riparian woodland that serves as a migrant trap in spring and is where many migrants can be found in season. Nesting species include all of those described above and more. Listen for the chatter of house wrens and the lively repetitions of warbling vireos. The chokecherry thickets that begin just beyond the woods should have yellow-breasted chat, yellow warbler, and broad-tailed hummingbird males, who are loafing and feeding while the females are tending nests and raising young. Check the brushy hillsides for both towhees and lesser goldfinches.

After a quarter mile of straightaway, the trail makes an abrupt double bend and crosses Van Bibber Creek. The dense, moist thickets in this area are a good place to look for MacGillivray's warbler and Cordilleran flycatcher. Check the creek for any species coming in for a drink. In season, the muddy areas here (and elsewhere in the park) also attract a variety of butterflies.

Past the creek, the trail begins a gradual ascent through open brushy hillsides, good for both towhees, western meadowlark, blue-gray gnatcatcher, Virginia's warbler, and yellow-breasted chat. Mountain bluebirds can often be seen flycatching in the meadows. If you wish to speed things up a bit, the next mile or so is a good place to do so as the habitat remains the same throughout this stretch and the trail becomes steeper and rocky. Ponderosa pines appear and become numerous as you ascend. Upon reaching the junction of the Belcher Hill and Mustang Trails, you have completed the most difficult part of the hike. You will find a bench at this spot to take a break and see what birds might come if you just sit for a while. From here, the trail levels out and the remainder of the hike is relatively easy. This provides an opportunity to walk slowly among the pines and watch for some of the coniferous forest specialties, including pine siskin, all three nuthatches, Steller's jay, hairy woodpecker, western tanager, and western wood-pewee. Northern goshawk is possible here, though seeing one requires some luck.

The trailhead at Lower White Ranch

Green-tailed towhee

You will soon arrive at a three-way intersection. Belcher Hill Trail divides the north and south sections of the Sawmill Trail Loop. All of these reach the same destination at the upper parking lot, but the route described here follows the north (right) portion of the Sawmill Trail. The trail continues through pine forest and margins of mountain prairie, where bird species are much the same as we have seen and will be found at the upper areas of the park. In the prairie areas, watch for western and mountain bluebirds.

Upon reaching the upper terminus of the trails, additional birding may be added by taking all or part of the Rawhide Trail loop. This area is especially good for red crossbill in all seasons, especially in years of good cone crop. Other higher-elevation species, such as pine grosbeak and red-naped sapsucker, are possible here, but tend to be few and far between.

The descent follows the upper Longhorn Trail to where it becomes bike-only. Here the Longhorn joins the Shorthorn Trail for hikers, which in a mile joins the lower Longhorn Trail. This will converge with the Belcher Hill Trail for the final mile of our hike. The route down passes through the same habitats as the ascent. Particular attention should be paid to the dense, moist thickets where the trail crosses drainages; these are good places to look for species that you may have missed on the way up, including lazuli bunting; MacGillivray's, Virginia's, and yellow warbler; and black-headed grosbeak.

The Longhorn Trail rejoins the Belcher Hill Trail to close the loop, and the last portion of the hike is a repeat of the beginning.

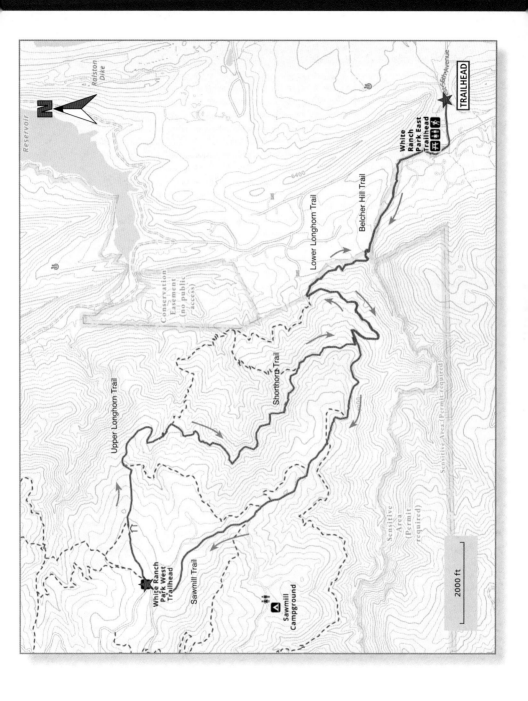

WHITE RANCH PARK

Chapter 12. **Rocky Mountain Arsenal**

ROUND-TRIP DISTANCE	4.7 miles
ELEVATION GAIN	Minimal
MAX ELEVATION	5,259 feet
TRAIL TYPE	Loop
DIFFICULTY	Easy
BEST SEASON(S)	Spring and fall

FEATURED BIRDS: Wintering bald eagles and summering burrowing owls, ducks, grebes, great blue heron, double-crested cormorant, gulls, shorebirds, and many songbirds including sparrows, warblers, flycatchers, wrens, and more

COMMENT: Rocky Mountain Arsenal has an interesting and controversial history. First established at the beginning of World War II as a munitions factory, it has seen the manufacture of explosives, poison gas, and, later, pesticides. Inadequate disposal procedures produced an extreme amount of pollution, and the Arsenal subsequently became a Superfund site. Following a lengthy cleanup, Rocky Mountain Arsenal became a National Wildlife Refuge.

The area is primarily prairie interspersed with lakes and woodlands. It is flat except for the large hummocks in the middle of the Wildlife Drive area, where the excavated polluted earth is buried.

The viewing blind

I recommend picking up a map of the property at the visitor center or printing a refuge map found online.

GETTING THERE: Take I-70 from either the west or east to the Quebec Street exit. Go north on Quebec to 64th Ave., which serves as the entrance to the Arsenal. Take 64th east for 0.6 mile and go north (left) on Gateway Rd. This will take you to the visitor center, where maps and other information are available.

THE ROUTE: Our hike begins at the parking area (restrooms) southwest of Lake Ladora. Take the trail that goes northeast toward the lake. It is at this point that our trail loop begins and closes. As with all loop trails, it can be run either direction, but in my opinion it is more interesting to begin with the loop around Lake Ladora. Bear left at the fork, and proceed along the trail that follows the shore of the lake. Along the southwest margin of Lake Ladora are numerous cottonwoods that should be checked for migrant songbirds in season. Once the trail clears the trees, it joins the road (closed to traffic) that connects the Wildlife Drive to the Lakes Ladora and Mary parking lot. Follow the road as it passes the parking lot and begins the loop around Lake Ladora. From this point until leaving Ladora, you will have good views of the lake, especially from the dam area near the parking lot. In spring and fall, the

Some of the local residents

Burrowing owl

lake may host hundreds of waterfowl, including most dabbling and diving ducks that nest or migrate through Colorado, Canada and cackling geese (sometimes with Ross's, snow, and greater white-fronted geese), grebes (horned, eared, pied-billed, western, and Clark's), double-crested cormorant, American coot, waders (including great blue heron, snowy egret, and great egret), marsh wren, and sora or Virginia rail in the marshes surrounding parts of the lake.

At the 1.6-mile mark, as you finish the loop around the lake, there is a metal footbridge that provides access across a marsh to Wildlife Drive. Crossing this bridge affords an opportunity to scan the margins of the cattails for rails and check any mudflats that may be exposed for shorebirds. In spring, red-winged and yellow-headed blackbirds abound. Watch and listen for marsh wrens.

Past the footbridge, the trail connects with Wildlife Drive. This hike combines several trails, and at this point following the road to the east will enable you to access the Rod and Gun Club, Woodland, and Prairie Trails. Continue east on Wildlife Drive and at 2.4 miles there is a parking lot on the south side of the road and an observation deck on the north. From this deck there are sweeping views of Lower Derby Lake, which in migration can be spectacular. The lake itself can have all of the species referenced for Lake Ladora. Mudflat and shoreline near the deck can have shorebirds, including American avocet, black-necked stilt, killdeer, and many more. American white pelicans can number into the hundreds here. Scan the cottonwood gallery on the north side of the lake; there are usually several bald eagles roosting there, especially in late fall and winter. Belted kingfishers patrol from perches along the banks, and western wood-pewees sally out and back from nearby cottonwoods.

Investigate the lake, then cross the road to the south and follow the paved path for a quarter mile. A short spur to the left takes you to a blind from which you can observe the Rod and Gun Club Ponds. These ponds host many dabbling ducks, such

Eared grebe

Cattail marsh in wooded prairie

as mallard, northern shoveler, gadwall, green-winged teal, and in summer, blue-winged and cinnamon teal. The ponds are shallow, actually more like ephemeral playas, and frequently have extensive mudflats. In migration, look for long-billed dowitcher, avocet, stilt, peep sandpipers, and more.

After checking the ponds, continue on the trail to the southwest. This is the Rod and Gun Club Trail, and soon it splits and then rejoins. The north branch skirts a cottonwood grove and passes through prairie, while the south branch passes through a locust grove. After the branches rejoin, the trail bears due west and passes through moderately wooded prairie. Check all along the trail for migrants in season.

At the 3.6-mile mark, you will arrive at the intersection of four trails: the Rod and Gun Club Trail that you have just completed, the Havana Ponds Trail, the Prairie Trail, and the Woodland Trail. If you wish to make a short detour, the Havana Ponds to the south (left) are worth checking for additional waterfowl and shorebirds. Go straight ahead to go along the Prairie Trail, which is repetitive of habitat already seen and dominates the rest of the Arsenal. Our route takes the Woodland Trail to the north (right). Immediately after making the turn, there is a small ditch that usually has some water. Check the brushy area around the ditch for migrants and water-loving summer residents like gray catbird.

Grasshopper sparrow

Two hundred yards beyond the ditch you will find a small pond on the east (right) side of the trail. This pond can be a real migrant magnet and should be checked carefully. In late summer/early fall, as the water evaporates and the pond shrinks, much mudflat is exposed and can host a variety of shorebirds. Wilson's phalaropes are often seen working the pond for prey items and any of the dabbling ducks, geese, and waders may be found here.

About a half mile from the intersection, the Woodland Trail crosses Wildlife Drive and skirts the edge of Lake Ladora. Follow it for a quarter mile to the fork where our loop began and now closes. Take the same trail we used earlier to return to the parking lot and finish the hike.

Suggestion: After completing the hike, take the Wildlife Drive, which makes an eleven-mile loop around the refuge. The first part of the drive features some marshes and woods that have potential for the same species as seen along our hike, and the remainder crosses large tracts of prairie where raptors cruise the skies. On the straightaway of the northernmost part of the drive, you will pass a small cottonwood grove and a deep drainage ditch. This area has recently proved good for grasshopper sparrow. At the northwest corner of the loop is a huge prairie dog town, which usually hosts a few burrowing owls.

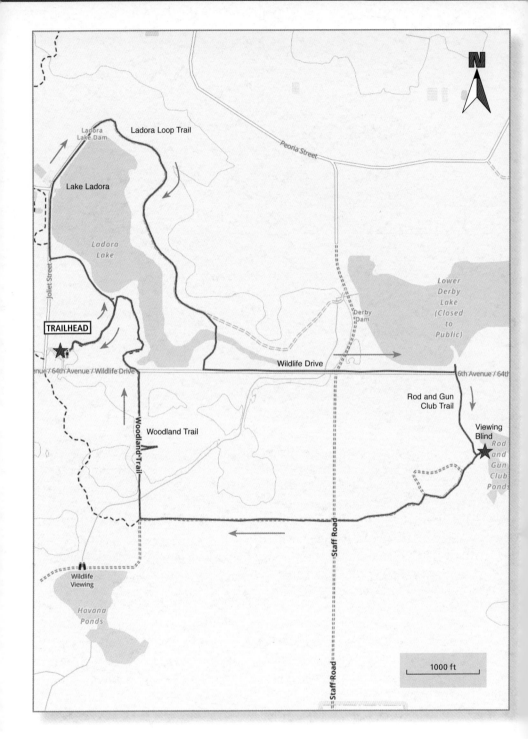

ROCKY MOUNTAIN ARSENAL

Chapter 13. **Bluff Lake**

ROUND-TRIP DISTANCE	1.5 miles
ELEVATION GAIN	150 feet
MAX ELEVATION	5,331 feet
TRAIL TYPE	Loop
DIFFICULTY	Easy
BEST SEASON(S)	Spring and fall

FEATURED BIRDS: Pied-billed grebe, Virginia rail, sora, snowy egret, black-crowned night-heron, great blue heron, wood duck, blue-winged teal, cinnamon teal, black-chinned hummingbird, western wood-pewee, Pay's phoebe, warbling vireo, Bullock's oriole, bald eagle, American tree sparrow, white-crowned sparrow, Harris's sparrow, belted kingfisher, American goldfinch, song sparrow, and wild turkeys

COMMENT: The Bluff Lake Nature Center is a self-contained unit that has changed ownership many times over the last century and a half. For most of the twentieth century, it was owned by Denver's Aviation Department and served as a crash zone at the end of the runways at the old Stapleton Airport. With the closing of the airport in 1995, the property found its way into the hands of Friends of Bluff Lake, who continue to manage it as a recreational and educational resource. It is an urban gem in the midst of rampant development, and is included here as an easy hike and fine birding in an urban setting. In summer, the park can become very hot; it is best to hike and bird the area in the early morning.

GETTING THERE: Follow I-70 from the east or west, or I-270 from the north, to Exit 279, Central Park Blvd. Go south on Central Park for 1.3 miles to Martin Luther King Jr. Blvd. Go left (east) at MLK for 1.8 miles to the visitor center and parking lot for Bluff Lake.

THE ROUTE: Our hike begins at the information kiosk adjacent to the parking

Great-tailed grackle at the marsh

Double-crested cormorants on their favorite roost snag in the lake

lot. Take any of the short trails through scrub habitat to the lengthy stairway that leads to the lake basin below. Before descending to the lake, check the scrub gardens for sparrows, especially in winter. Harris's sparrow is occasionally found here. Upon reaching the bottom of the steps, you will arrive at the amphitheater and the inter-section of several trails. A short trail leads to the right (east) and ends at a stream drop structure on Sand Creek, which is a good area to check for ducks and other

Lake, marsh, and woodlands in the late summer

Yellow warbler with lunch by the lake

waterfowl. The riparian cottonwoods are a frequent nesting site for Bullock's oriole. The short spur to the north also provides views of the creek.

As the trails in the park are not currently named, we will refer to them as the "Main Trail" and the "Sand Creek Loop." Take the Main Trail to the northwest for a couple hundred yards until you reach an intersection. This is the Sand Creek Spur, which meanders for a half mile roughly parallel to Sand Creek. The trail passes through scrubby woodland, which is a good place to look for one of the specialties of the park: black-chinned hummingbird. In spring, while abundant broad-tailed hummingbirds move to the mountains to breed, the black-chins remain behind in their preferred arid habitats. Two-thirds of the way around the loop, another trail splits off to the northwest. This is the Sand Creek Spur, which passes through more grassy scrub and can be worth checking for sparrows. Return to the loop and follow the trail until it rejoins the Main Trail. At this point you will find a boardwalk that extends out into a large marsh and provides an opportunity to view ducks, grebes, geese, great blue heron, double-crested cormorant, and other waterfowl. The cattails along the boardwalk abound with blackbirds. Listen here for the "witchity" song of the common yellowthroat. Virginia rail and sora are frequently heard, and sometimes seen, from the boardwalk.

Returning to the trail, you will pass through a small prairie and arrive at the cottonwood gallery on the north side of Bluff Lake. Numerous species nest here, including house wren, Bullock's oriole, yellow warbler, downy woodpecker, and others. All six of Colorado's common swallows (barn, cliff, tree, violet-green, northern rough-winged, and bank) can be seen cruising the surface of the lake. Reaching the turn at the west end of the lake, you will find the bird blind. This is a fine spot to take a break and watch waterfowl, swallows, and songbirds from behind the wall of the blind. In summer, the stagnant water near the blind also has much to offer the dragonfly enthusiast.

As the trail rounds the west end of the lake and starts the final half mile back to the trailhead, it rises a bit and follows the bluff that gives the lake its name. The habitat is arid and less vegetated than the areas nearer the lake, and can be a good place to find Say's phoebe, western kingbird, blue grosbeak, and other species that prefer a more open upland environment. The bluff portion of the trail passes along the south margin of the lake, and the elevation provides superb views of any birds on the lake. Check among the cattails for American coot, blue-winged and cinnamon teal, and perching song sparrow.

Continue along the Main Trail as it follows the bluff to the east and eventually curves to the north and closes the loop at the amphitheater.

The boardwalk through the marsh

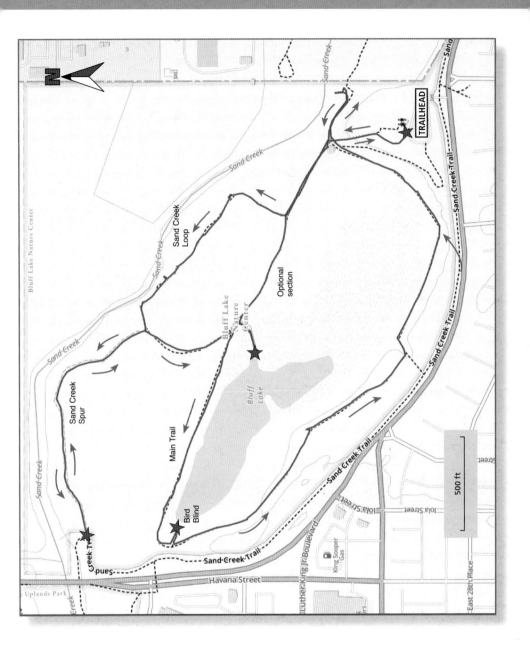

BLUFF LAKE

Chapter 14. **Clear Creek Trail**

ROUND-TRIP DISTANCE	15 miles
ELEVATION GAIN	603 feet
MAX ELEVATION	5,740 feet
TRAIL TYPE	Out-and-back or drive-and-drop
DIFFICULTY	Moderate
BEST SEASON(S)	Spring

FEATURED BIRDS: Blackpoll; yellow, yellow-rumped, Townsend's, McGilli-vray's, Wilson's, black-throated gray, palm, Tennessee, and magnolia warblers; belted kingfisher; Wilson's snipe; northern parula; American redstart; northern waterthrush; several species of Empidonax flycatchers; plumbeous, Cassin's, and warbling vireos; American tree and Lincoln's sparrows; western tanager; American goldfinch; song sparrow; spotted towhee; white-breasted nuthatch; Bullock's oriole; double-crested cormorant; great blue heron; cackling goose; grebes; and sandhill cranes

COMMENT: The Clear Creek Trail extends for twenty miles, from the South Platte River to Golden. The part of the trail described here begins at Kipling Street in the Wheat Ridge Greenbelt (City of Wheat Ridge) and continues in the greenbelt until it is completed with the final stretch from the west end of the greenbelt to Golden.

Winter visitor—American tree sparrow

Along the way, it winds through Prospect Park and riparian woodlands, passes several lakes and a large marsh (Prospect Lake, Bass Lake, Tabor Lake, and West Lake), and finally ends in an industrial/commercial district and urban park. Consequently, the trail offers a variety of habitats and has become well-known over the years for the numbers of migrant and resident birds that can be observed along it. It is known for hosting a few unusual warblers every spring and is part of the Colorado Birding Trail.

GETTING THERE: Access Kipling Street from either the north or south. The parking lot for the Wheat Ridge Greenbelt is on the west side of Kipling, 0.2 mile north of 41st Ave.

Island in Tabor Lake with cormorant/heron colony

THE ROUTE: Beginning at the Kipling parking lot, the hiker is soon given a choice: you can follow the paved multiuse trail on the north side of Clear Creek or take the unpaved trail on the south side. Each has its advantages. The paved path makes for easier walking and has numerous points where the hiker can access the creek. The unpaved trail on the south side of the creek tends to hang somewhat closer to the creek and has the additional benefit of passing near some willow thickets that are favored by migrant songbirds. This description will follow the paved path on the north side of the creek.

The trail meanders through cottonwood riparian habitat for a half mile. In summer, look for Bullock's orioles, which nest here in numbers. In some of the moist woodlands there should be yellow warbler and gray catbird.

At three-quarters of a mile you will find a small man-made rapid/waterfall. This is a good place to look for spotted sandpiper. Anywhere there are (what pass for) rapids on Clear Creek, check for American dipper. These little birds, with dense feathers that flash white nictitating membranes, make a habit of standing on rocks doing knee bends. They prefer rocky stretches of the creek with swirling water. Watch them completely submerge as they browse the streambed for invertebrates, then pop out like a cork onto a rock perch. In winter, you are

Wood duck

Green-winged teal

almost certain to see one along the creek. Rocks with whitewash are an indication that a dipper has been there.

A mile in from the trailhead you will reach a footbridge across the creek. This bridge offers one of several alternative routes along the trail. This description will follow the improved path along the north side of the creek, but crossing to the south side also offers a variety of habitats.

At the bridge, you have also reached the parking lot for Prospect Park and Lake. At the west end of the lot, pause for a few minutes and scan Prospect Lake. In winter there can be lots of Canada and cackling geese, large numbers of northern shovelers are often here, and common goldeneye and hooded merganser seem to favor this lake. It should be noted that most birders begin their visit to the greenbelt here. Prospect Park offers another option for hiking and birding selected portions of the trail.

Continuing along the trail, in another quarter mile you will arrive at Tabor Lake, which usually has a variety of dabbling and diving ducks, pied-billed grebe in all seasons, and horned, eared, and western grebes in migration. The main attraction here, however, is the small island in the middle of the lake. This island hosts a mixed colony of nesting double-crested cormorants and great blue herons in the trees, with a few Canada geese using the ground. Black-crowned night-heron is sometimes seen here too.

At the west end of Tabor Lake is the third footbridge. This is an excellent vantage point from which to scan for dippers, and there are usually mallard and gadwall in the creek below. Also check for a kingfisher perching in overhanging branches.

Cross the bridge and turn left. Walk east for fifty yards and turn right onto the trail that passes along the west side of Bass Lake. Surrounding the lake is an extensive cattail marsh that hosts red-winged and yellow-headed blackbirds in summer. Watch and listen for marsh wren and song sparrow.

The trail makes a loop around Bass Lake (the Bass Lake Nature Trail). Continuing south, you will soon come to a bend that will take you to a boardwalk along the south side of the lake. This is a good place to watch and listen for the descending whinny of a sora or the strange grunting call of Virginia rail. Common yellowthroat nest in these cattails. Follow this trail until it circles

American dipper

back around the north side of Bass Lake and rejoins the main trail, and return to the westbound route. West Lake is now on the south side of the trail, and it offers another opportunity to see waterfowl. Ring-billed gulls favor this lake.

At the 2.5-mile mark, the trail passes under I-70. Just beyond the overpass is a popular gold-panning area. This stretch of rapidly flowing creek also appeals to goldeneye, hooded and common merganser (winter), and scads of mallards, gadwall, and green-winged teal. The trail hugs the creek for the next half mile. This is a good stretch in which to check for snipe. Swamp sparrow is also seen here in winter.

The trail then makes a ninety-degree turn to the north and crosses the fourth bridge. Pause and check the ponded water and the surrounding vegetation for waterfowl and sparrows in winter. Continue across the bridge and the trail turns west again. Watch the gravel bars along the creek for snipe and killdeer in winter. Rusty blackbird and snow bunting have been seen here. The path then passes under the railroad tracks. On the other side, a few Russian olive trees begin to appear. In winter, check them for waxwings and robins. Warblers, vireos, thrushes, and flycatchers may be seen in migration. There is a series of artificial ponds on the south side of the creek that may yield some ducks or grebes.

At the 4.1-mile mark is an isolated marshy woodland thicket. This is a fine spot to check again for thrushes and bug-eating passerines (warblers, vireos, flycatchers) in migration. Just beyond this woodland you will pass the first of many buildings of the vast Coors Brewing Company (now Molson-Coors, but to locals it will always be Coors). At 4.5 miles, the trail will pass under McIntyre Street. Just beyond the

Snow bunting, a winter rarity

overpass, North and South Table Mountains (actually basalt-capped mesas) come into view. Golden eagles nest on the cliffs of North Table Mountain, and for the rest of our hike raptors are likely to be the stars of the show. Red-tailed (all seasons), Swainson's (summer), and rough-legged (winter) hawks frequent the area. American kestrel (our smallest falcon), prairie, and peregrine falcon are also possible.

Except for raptors, the next mile of trail is not likely to be particularly birdy, so this is a good time to take off your birding hat, put on your hiking hat, and make some time. At the 6-mile mark, the trail ascends a high overpass across 44th Avenue, which is also the high point of the trail at 5,740 feet. At this point you are across Clear Creek from the massive Coors Brewery. Need a pigeon for the day's list? This is a good place to pick one up. Beyond the overpass the trail runs past a few scattered woodlands that might have a bird or two. Be sure to check the towering basalt cliffs above for raptors and acrobatic white-throated swifts in the summer.

At 7.5 miles, the trail makes a hairpin turn to the south and follows a small tributary creek within a containment channel. Check along this little creek for spotted sandpiper. The trail then crosses 10th Street. Eighty yards past 10th Street, take a sharp right across a small bridge, and you will find yourself at Andover Park, the terminus of our hike. At the south side of the park is another opportunity to check Clear Creek for more birds. The Clear Creek Trail continues through Golden toward the west, but our hike ends here.

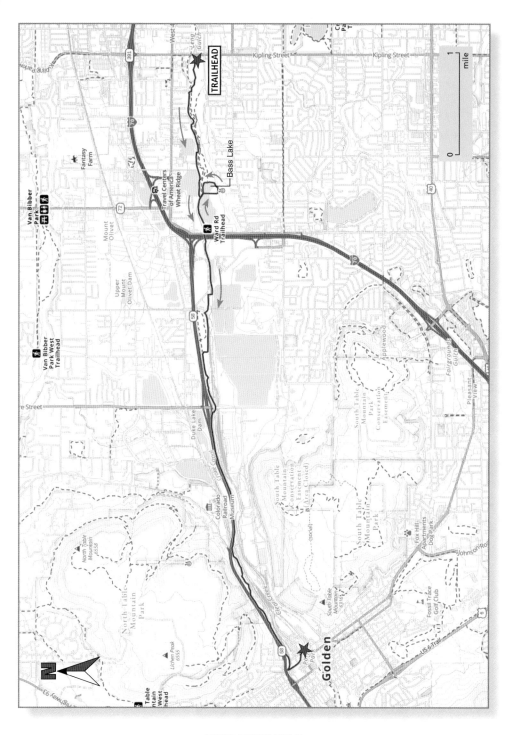

CLEAR CREEK TRAIL

Chapter 15. **Genesee Mountain Park**

ROUND-TRIP DISTANCE	1.25 miles
ELEVATION GAIN	246 feet
MAX ELEVATION	8,269 feet
TRAIL TYPE	Loop
DIFFICULTY	Easy
BEST SEASON(S)	Summer and early fall

FEATURED BIRDS: Williamson's sapsucker; tree and violet-green swallows; pygmy, white-breasted, and red-breasted nuthatches; brown creeper; mountain chickadee; mountain and western bluebirds; chipping sparrow; western tanager; and red crossbill

COMMENT: Genesee Mountain Park is a Denver Mountain Park situated in Jefferson County. It is among the easiest of our hikes but also one of the most productive. It can be good at any season, but is best during summer nesting season and migration in late summer/early fall, when mountain species are descending from higher elevations.

Western tanager

GETTING THERE: Travel up I-70 from the Denver area west into the foothills and take the Genesee exit. At the top of the exit ramp, you may see the resident bison herd in the meadows on either side of I-70. After looking at the bison, turn left, and follow the road as it crosses I-70. After crossing over I-70, you will come to an intersection. Turn right and follow Genesee Mountain Road as it winds its way up to the park. Soon you will arrive at the main parking lot. The road continues up the mountain, but is gated at the picnic area, so park and begin the hike.

Pygmy nuthatch at nest cavity in the "wildlife tree"

THE ROUTE: Begin the hike at the large parking lot. After walking north out of the parking lot, note the broken tree to the west of the picnic area. It is perforated with woodpecker holes, which serve as nesting cavities for pygmy nuthatches, tree swallows, and other birds. It has a small plaque designating it as a "wildlife tree." The picnic area has pygmy nuthatches—listen for their incessant peeping. Williamson's sapsucker is also frequently seen here, as well as hairy woodpecker and dark-eyed junco. Continue hiking up the paved road, where you may find all the nuthatches and brown creepers working the ponderosa pines. After about a hundred yards, you will come to a small open prairie area on the left. This and other similar open areas are good for bluebirds. Broad-tailed humming-birds abound among the scattered blooming bushes in late summer.

Broad-tailed hummingbird

Continue following the road as the pavement ends and the dirt/

Signature species—Williamson's sapsucker   "Audubon's" yellow-rumped warbler

gravel portion begins. Look among the variety of conifers for dark-eyed juncos, red crossbills, Hammond's flycatcher, chipping sparrow, and mountain and western bluebirds (summer). Listen for the "Quick! Three beers!" song of the olive-sided flycatcher. The road circles the mountain, taking a corkscrew route up to the top. As you round the north end of the circle, you will enter an area that is favored by western tanagers as Mount Evans comes into view. A little farther up the road is the upper parking area. Check the cavities in the ponderosa pines for nesting bluebirds, and this is another area frequented by Williamson's sapsucker.

Upon reaching the parking area, proceed up the path at the far end of the lot to the top of Genesee Mountain. The top is marked by a flagpole that was erected by the Daughters of the American Revolution over a century ago. There is a small open area at the summit. At the end opposite the flagpole is a

White-breasted nuthatch

The trail winds its way up the mountain

dead ponderosa pine, which is riddled with woodpecker holes. This is the "condo tree" and it hosts nesting swallows, nuthatches, and woodpeckers. Rock wrens can sometimes be found among the small rock outcroppings in this area.

You can take the road back down or descend via the Genesee Mountain Trail, found midway along the parking area. In the open woodlands along this trail many species are found, including western bluebird, Williamson's sapsucker, brown creeper, all three nuthatches, northern flicker, American robin, broad-tailed hummingbird (late summer), and yellow-rumped warbler (late summer). Listen for the raspy up-and-down song of the plumbeous vireo and scan the sky for a soaring red-tailed hawk or turkey vulture. In this type of habitat, listen for subtle pecking sounds, which can lead you to nuthatches or woodpeckers (Williamson's and red-naped sapsuckers, downy or hairy woodpeckers, and northern flicker).

Upon reaching the road, take a short walk around the group picnic pavilion. Williamson's sapsuckers are found here and Cassin's finches sing from the tops of the ponderosas. In the open field adjacent to the pavilion, look for both bluebirds, chipping sparrow, American robin, and dark-eyed junco.

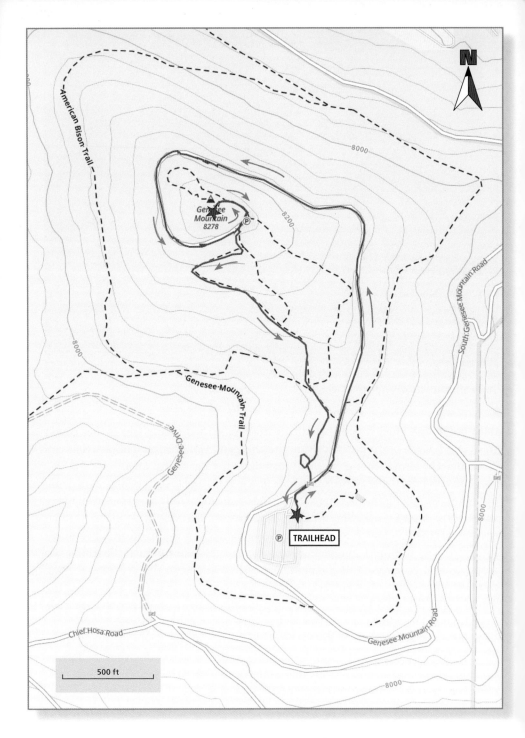

GENESEE MOUNTAIN PARK

Chapter 16. Red Rocks/ Matthews-Winters Park

ROUND-TRIP DISTANCE	8 miles
ELEVATION GAIN	500 feet
MAX ELEVATION	6,400 feet
TRAIL TYPE	Out-and-back or drive-and-drop
DIFFICULTY	Moderate
BEST SEASON(S)	All

FEATURED BIRDS: Black-capped and mountain chickadees, Woodhouse's scrub-jay, canyon wren, Townsend's solitaire, white-crowned sparrow, black-headed grosbeak, spotted and green-tailed towhees, indigo (rare) and lazuli buntings, yellow-breasted chat, Bullock's oriole, white-breasted swift, violet-green swallow, dark-eyed junco, peregrine falcons, prairie falcon, barn owl, and common raven

COMMENT: Red Rocks is home to the world-famous Red Rocks Amphitheatre, where hundreds of musicians have performed across the decades. The key to the setting of the park and amphitheater is its spectacular geology. The name "Red Rocks" is derived from the red strata of the Fountain Formation, which is a continental (non-oceanic) sediment formed from the erosion of the Ancestral Rockies about 300 million years ago. During the period of mountain building that resulted in the present Rocky Mountains, the layers of the Fountain Formation were uplifted near the mountain front, which resulted in the angled flatiron configuration that we see today. In addition, while you are hiking, look to the east at the hogback. While the hogback is capped with a hard sandstone called the Dakota Formation, the west side of the ridge, which is visible from Red Rocks, is composed of another complex of continental sediments, the Morrison Formation. This famous formation has yielded numerous dinosaur remains over the years.

Within the park you will not find a wide variety of habitats; it is entirely foothills scrub/prairie and rock outcroppings with a few small groves of trees. There is a little more woodland near the parking lot for Matthews-Winters Park. This hike works well as a "drive-and-drop," with hikers teaming up to leave a car at one trailhead and start the hike at the other.

Cassin's finch

Dark-eyed junco

GETTING THERE: Trailheads for this hike can be accessed from either Red Rocks Park (you will hike uphill) or Matthews-Winters Park (you will hike downhill).

To begin at Red Rocks Park, take C-470 to the Morrison exit, and go west. Pass through Morrison on Bear Creek Ave. You will reach a traffic light (Maple St.) at the west end of town. Proceed through this intersection and take the next right into the park on Red Rocks Park Road. In a quarter mile, there is a fork in the road. Stay right, and the parking lot for the route will be on your immediate right.

To begin at Matthews-Winters Park, take I-70 west from Denver until you pass through the impressive road cut at the hogback, a.k.a. Dakota Ridge or Dinosaur Ridge. Take the next exit toward Morrison to the south. Go a quarter mile to the entrance to the park on the right.

THE ROUTE: Assuming that you have chosen to do the uphill version of this hike, our hike begins at the Red Rocks parking lot as previously described. Before crossing the road to the west, check the large monolith to the north of the parking lot. Barn owls have nested in crevices near the base and prairie falcons are frequently seen perched on ledges of the rock. Proceed across the road and follow the Trading Post Trail as it rounds the corner of another large rock formation and heads northwest. During spring weather events, the prairies around this part of the trail sometimes experience fallouts of yellow-rumped warblers and mountain and western bluebirds.

Continue for a quarter mile to where the trail takes a small bend to the east and passes the west face of Frog Rock (where it splits and rejoins; either option is fine), followed by another turn to the northwest. Here the trail enters a small wooded canyon that runs along the base of Nine Parks Rock. This narrow canyon can be a treasure trove of migrants and summer residents. Look here in spring and summer for black-headed grosbeak, Bullock's oriole, black-capped chickadee, yellow warbler, and downy woodpecker. Watch the rocks above and listen for the marvelous cascading song of the canyon wren. When you emerge from the north end of the canyon, you will find yourself on Ship Rock Road.

While in Red Rocks Park, our route will follow park roads for a couple of stretches. In this area there are also a couple of opportunities for short side expeditions, if you so desire. The first presents itself as you arrive at Ship Rock Road. The trail follows the road to the north, but I recommend a short walk across the road and onto the Upper South Parking Lot. Proceed to the northwest corner of the lot, which will put you southwest of Ship Rock, where there is a nice array of junipers and deciduous scrub. In winter, this is a favorite site for Townsend's solitaires, which take advantage of the juniper berry crop. Steller's jays frequently venture down from the mountains and can be seen here. In the warmer months, scan the upper parts of the rock for the peregrine falcons that have nested here for years, as well as for common ravens, which also use the rock for their large stick nests. There will often be clouds of violet-green and tree swallows, as well as white-throated swifts hunting around the tops of Ship Rock and its neighbor to the north of the amphitheater, Creation Rock.

Woodhouse's scrub-jay

Peregrine falcon nest site

Deciduous forest in the valley west of Frog Rock

Return to the trail and continue north for a short distance until you come to a rock stairway on the right side of the trail, another side opportunity. This path will take you to the Trading Post, now home to the Colorado Music Hall of Fame. The Trading Post also features a dense thicket of scrub on its southwest side. This thicket is possibly the best place in the park to find Woodhouse's scrub-jay, though the jay is one of the most common birds in the park at all seasons. It also hosts house finches, mountain and black-capped chickadees, and spotted towhee. For years, birders kept this area stocked with seed in winter, but park policy on this has changed in recent years. When the feeders are active in winter, juncos of all five common flavors are found here in abundance, scrub-jays seem to be everywhere, and numerous rarities have appeared at times. These have included curve-billed thrasher, golden-crowned sparrow, fox sparrow, and others.

If you indulge in this detour, return to the trail/road and turn left at the stop sign onto Trading Post Road. Our route follows the road for a little over a quarter mile and then leaves the road to make a sharp turn to the southeast, followed by a hairpin turn back to the north. In this area, the habitat is open prairie with scattered scrub. This is a good place to check for lazuli and indigo (rare) buntings, western meadowlark, Say's phoebe, and sage thrasher in migration. At the trail junction, stay to the left and continue north. The trail follows Red Rocks Trail on the road for a bit and then crosses West Alameda Parkway. Here we leave the roads of Red Rocks and continue north up a gradual rise. We soon come to the intersection of the Red Rocks and Morrison Slide Trails. Either will work; the Morrison Slide will take you up some switchbacks to a slightly higher elevation, while Red Rocks continues more or less straight to the north. Each passes through prairie with scattered scrub, and both are good places to look for scrub specialists like spotted and green-tailed towhees, bushtit, blue-gray gnatcatcher, Virginia's warbler, and black-headed grosbeak.

Along the way, you will pass from Red Rocks into Matthews-Winters Park. In a half mile the trail splits into Village Walk to the left (west) and Village Ride to the south (right). They rejoin at the parking lot, so take either and watch and listen for rock wren around some of the outcrops. The trails cross Mount Vernon Creek near the end of our route and pass through a riparian area, which is the only site along the trail that might have water. The riparian woodland around the creek is a great spot to check for birds of that habitat, including western wood-pewee, least and Cordilleran flycatchers, western kingbird, warbling vireo, lesser goldfinch, song sparrow, yellow warbler, and yellow-breasted chat.

Our hike ends at the parking lot, if you have left a car here. Otherwise, you can return via the same route, and perhaps take a few of the trail options that you did not choose on the way up.

Ship Rock, where falcons, ravens, swifts, and canyon wrens nest

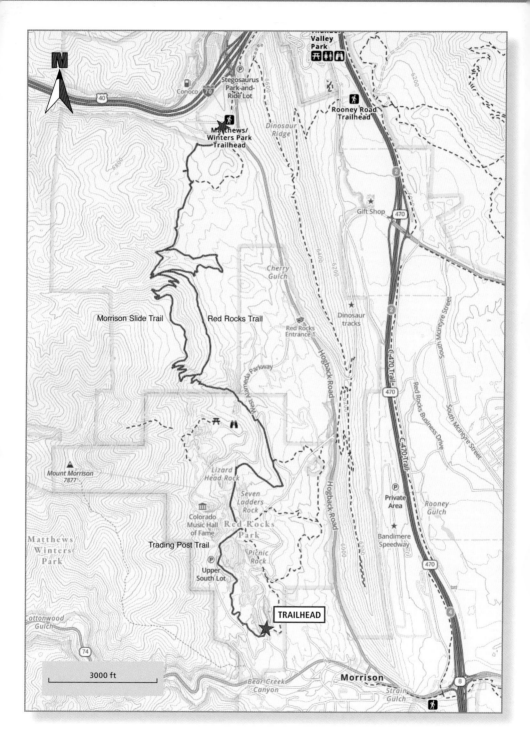

RED ROCKS/MATTHEWS-WINTERS PARK

Chapter 17. **Lair o' the Bear**

ROUND-TRIP DISTANCE	2.3 miles
ELEVATION GAIN	300 feet
MAX ELEVATION	6,725 feet
TRAIL TYPE	Loop
DIFFICULTY	Easy
BEST SEASON(S)	Summer

FEATURED BIRDS: Western wood-pewee, Cordilleran flycatcher, blue-gray gnatcatcher, plumbeous and warbling vireos, American dipper, cedar waxwing, Townsend's solitaire, MacGillivray's and Virginia's warblers, chipping and song sparrows, black-headed grosbeak, lazuli bunting, and lesser goldfinch

COMMENT: Lair o' the Bear Park is an excellent birding area due to the unusual variety of habitats in a small area, accessible by several trails. The hike described here will cross small prairies, follow a creekside riparian corridor, ascend through brushy hillsides, and top out in coniferous forest, all within less than a mile of the starting point.

GETTING THERE: On the west side of the Denver area, take C-470 to the Morrison exit and go west through the town of Morrison. In about four miles you will pass through the village of Idledale. Continue for another mile and you will see the corral-type entrance to this, a Jefferson County Open Space park.

THE ROUTE: Our hike begins by following the Bear Creek Trail to the east out of the parking area. After passing the restrooms on the left, the trail enters a small prairie where lazuli bunting and yellow warbler are often seen. Bear Creek is on the right. The willows lining the creek are home to song sparrows throughout the year. American dippers like this section of

Virginia's warbler

Bear Creek

creek, especially in winter, and in midsummer look for cedar waxwings flycatching over the water. As you approach the footbridge over Bear Creek, you will come to a stand of large willow trees. Before continuing, check these trees and the surrounding thickets. Virginia's warbler, warbling vireo, and gray catbird can often be found here.

Soon you will come to Ouzel Bridge over Bear Creek. Pause here in late summer to watch broad-tailed hummingbirds chasing gnats over the creek. This is also a popular spot for western wood-pewee, which can be found along the creek making its hunting flights out over the water. After crossing the bridge, you will find yourself at the intersection of two habitats; the large cottonwoods on the left host nesting Cordilleran flycatchers, while MacGillivray's warblers can be found in the moist thicket on the right.

Where the trail meets a junction at the rock face, you can follow Bear Creek Trail to the left toward Little Park in Idledale. This stretch of trail follows the creek and is active in summer and migration seasons. However, our route goes to the right and follows the Bruin Bluff Trail as it gradually ascends across brushy hillsides toward the ponderosa forest above. As you pass the thickets on the right side of the trail, be alert for the song of the elusive MacGillivray's warbler. Look for green-tailed and spotted towhees, mountain and black-capped chickadee, blue-gray gnatcatcher, and black-headed grosbeak among the rocks and bushes. The deciduous trees on the lower parts of the slope have nesting warbling vireos in summer, while

Ouzel Bridge

plumbeous vireo and western tanager can be found in the pine trees above. These pines also host mountain chickadee, pygmy nuthatch, and lesser goldfinch throughout the spring and summer. Where the trail traverses hillsides covered with mountain mahogany, look and listen for blue-gray gnatcatcher and Virginia's warbler. In winter, look for Townsend's solitaire perched at the top of junipers, giving its monotonous "toot" notes. Mountain chickadee and pygmy nuthatch are common in the conifers in all seasons.

Continue west on the trail as it undulates around several small valleys. You will alternate between sunny slopes with mountain mahogany and the interior of piney woodland. Among the pines, check for red-breasted nuthatch, brown creeper, dark-eyed junco, and various woodpeckers. Some of the areas along the trail afford good looks from above at the trees and bushes in the valley below. These can be fine spots to look for birds that perch high in the trees, but of course, the birder will be looking at them from eye level or above.

As the trail descends at the west end of the park, it rounds a wide turn back toward the east and passes several dead trees riddled with woodpecker holes. Look for house wrens and bluebirds nesting in these cavities. Where the trail runs along the creek, look for American dipper and song sparrow. Red-tailed hawks and sometimes golden eagles can be seen riding the updrafts from the canyon walls.

Soon you will reach a trail junction. To return directly to the parking area, take the left fork and cross Dipper Bridge, then bear right. You can take the main trail or investigate the creek further. The section of creek near the picnic area is good for belted kingfisher.

The right fork will take you along the Castor Cutoff, which follows the riparian vegetation for a bit then dips into a small, moist depression. Broad-tailed, calliope, and rufous hummingbirds have all been seen here in late summer. The trail crosses a grassy slope and rejoins the Bruin Bluff Trail, which you can follow by the same route (in reverse) that you followed earlier in the hike.

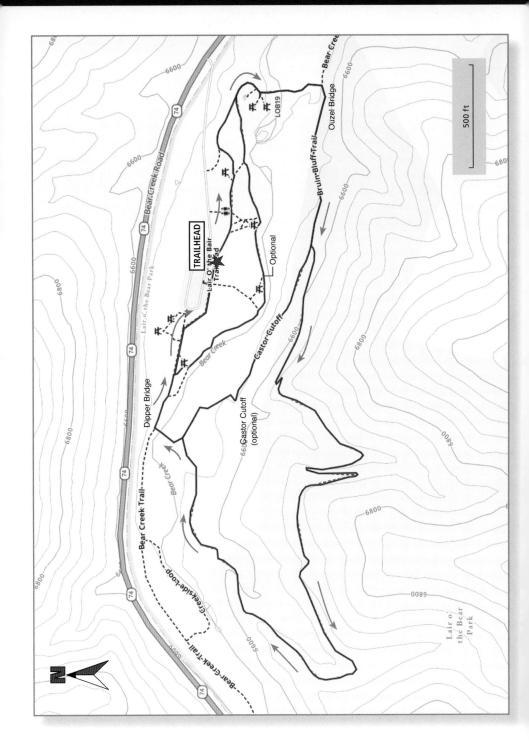

LAIR O' THE BEAR

Chapter 18. **Bear Creek Lake Park**

ROUND-TRIP DISTANCE	7.3 miles
ELEVATION GAIN	267 feet
MAX ELEVATION	5,767 feet
TRAIL TYPE	Loop
DIFFICULTY	Moderate
BEST SEASON(S)	Spring and summer

FEATURED BIRDS: Great horned owl, red-tailed hawk, green-tailed and spotted towhees, song sparrow, multiple corvids (common raven, American crow, black-billed magpie, Woodhouse's scrub-jay, and blue jay), western wood-pewee, Say's phoebe, Bullock's oriole, yellow warbler, cedar waxwing, black-headed grosbeak, lazuli bunting, and a wide array of waterfowl (double-crested cormorant, American white pelican, most dabbling and diving ducks, and pied-billed grebe), which appear at various seasons. American dipper, and several sparrow species: dark-eyed junco, white-crowned sparrow, American tree sparrow, and Harris's and swamp sparrows are rare but regular with a little searching. Townsend's solitaire; mountain and western bluebirds; tree swallow; western meadowlark; Swainson's and hermit thrushes; plumbeous and warbling vireos; yellow-rumped, Virginia's, and Wilson's warblers; broad-tailed hummingbird; clay-colored and Brewer's sparrows; dusky, Hammond's, and olive-sided flycatchers; and numerous shorebirds, including spotted sandpiper, American avocet, and Wilson's phalarope. American redstart, Tennessee, Nashville, chestnut-sided, blackpoll, and black-throated green warblers are among the more unusual warblers seen here occasionally.

COMMENT: This is a fee area. Bear Creek Lake Park is a City of Lakewood park; note that state park passes do not apply here. BCLP is almost identical in setting and habitats to nearby Chatfield State Park, also a popular birding destination. However, BCLP offers a much better system of trails than Chatfield, which has a few attractive trails but none that provide as productive a loop as the Mount Carbon Loop at BCLP. Our hike follows the Mountain Carbon Loop Trail for over half of its length, joining parts of the Cottonwood, Red Tail, and Owl Trails for its final third. Bear Creek Lake Park is a great migrant trap in both spring and fall.

GETTING THERE: From the east, take Morrison Road to the park entrance, about a half mile east of C-470. From the west, take C-470 to the Morrison exit. Turn left

Bear Creek Lake from the high point on Mount Carbon

(east) off the exit and go a half mile to the park entrance. Once in the park, turn right at the first intersection and proceed a short distance down the road to the Skunk Hollow parking area.

THE ROUTE: Begin at the Skunk Hollow parking lot and take the trail that goes east out of the lot. Cross the entrance road and make an immediate left turn, taking the bridge over Bear Creek. This is one of many opportunities to check the creek for American dipper, one of the signature birds of the park. After crossing the bridge, follow the trail to the right as it winds along a route paralleling the riparian woodlands on the right with meadows on the left. While passing through this area, look for migrants, bluebirds, Say's phoebe, and black-billed magpie in the meadows. In winter and early spring, look high in the cottonwoods for the great horned owls that frequently nest here.

At one-half mile there is a footbridge over a small brushy drainage. Check here for song sparrow and Wilson's, MacGillivray's, and yellow warblers. Just beyond the bridge is an artificial concrete waterfall. Spotted sandpiper can be seen here. Check the tall utility towers above for raptors. Another two hundred yards down the trail is a bridge across Bear Creek. Do not cross the bridge, but it is another good place to check for dipper.

At 1.1 miles, the trail intersects the creek with brushy riparian growth and low, overhanging trees. Take a few minutes to carefully check this area; it is a habitat for winter wren. A Pacific wren was found here in December of 2019.

The trail through a riparian area

At the 1.5-mile mark, the Mount Carbon Trail intersects with the Fisherman's Trail and makes a sharp left turn. However, proceed straight on Fisherman's, through a picnic ground, to the edge of the lake. There is a trail spur to the right. Follow it as it passes along lakeside brush, woodlands, and ends at an exposed point in the lake. This provides the first good opportunity to view waterfowl, depending upon the season. The habitat along the trail is excellent for ruby-crowned kinglet, song sparrow, and migrants in season. In winter, the area can abound with dark-eyed junco, American tree and white-crowned sparrows, and Harris's or white-throated sparrow might also be present. The lakeshore should have some shorebirds in fall and all six common swallow species in summer.

Around the picnic area, look for birds feeding on the ground including northern flicker, American robin, and song and white-crowned sparrows. Cross the footbridge at the east end of the picnic area and check the brushy ditch for birds. At the east end of the paved parking lot is another area that has had Harris's sparrow in winter and might be worth a look. Watch and listen for belted kingfisher at all seasons. There is also a restroom here.

Backtrack to the west via the road next to the restroom and rejoin the Mount Carbon Trail at the far end of the unpaved parking lot. In a few yards, the trail crosses the road where there is a footbridge across another small drainage. Each of these drainages should be checked for migrants and birds of brushy habitat. After crossing the bridge, bypass the fork to the left and at the next intersection bear right. This stretch of trail passes through yucca/rabbitbrush prairie and can have Say's phoebe, blue grosbeak, western meadowlark, and perhaps even a loggerhead (summer) or northern shrike (winter).

At 2.4 miles, the trail crosses another drainage and makes an abrupt left turn, beginning a long loop to the north that will eventually skirt the north end of the Mount Carbon Dam and turn back to the south. At the north end of this loop, the park maintains some rock piles for construction. Check these for rock wren in summer. If you wish, you can walk out onto the dam to scan for waterfowl, but our route bypasses the dam and begins a descent to the south, paralleling the dam. This section of the trail is not particularly interesting, as it passes between the grassy slope of the dam on the right and golf courses on the left. However, birds do not always respect what is appropriate habitat, so check the trees for a downy woodpecker or Bullock's oriole.

At 3.75 miles, the trail crosses a paved road and begins the ascent up Mount Carbon, which might be more appropriately called "Big Hill" Carbon. Whatever the case, as the trail climbs, it passes through thick brush of mountain mahogany and is perfect habitat for spotted and green-tailed towhees and Virginia's warbler. The summit of Large Mount Carbon is at 4.15 miles, a hospitable site. There is a picnic shelter, a restroom, and a bench. This is a great place to take a break and enjoy the views of the lake, the park, and the Front Range.

While the north slope of the hill is covered with brush, the west side is hot, arid, and populated by yucca and prairie dogs. Check on the way down for rock wren,

Mount Carbon

The trail up Mount Carbon passes through brushy hillside habitat

Say's phoebe, and in migration, sage thrasher. The area is a bit busy for their liking, but it can't hurt to check the prairie dog colony for burrowing owl.

As the trail levels at the bottom of the hill, a short stretch deviates to the right and hugs the shoreline for a quarter mile before rejoining the main trail. Here there is a quiet corner of the lake that is good for double-crested cormorant, great blue heron, dabbling ducks (mallard, wigeon, gadwall), and shorebirds in fall.

Stay right at the fork and you will come to another small creek. The willows along the creek are a great place to find song and white-crowned sparrows or a warbler in migration. A bit beyond the bridge over the creek, the Mount Carbon Trail meets the Cottonwood Trail. Take Cottonwood Trail to the right and check the marsh for teal, red-winged blackbird, and marsh wren. Virginia rail and sora have been found here.

Continue on the Cottonwood Trail around the small knoll to Pelican Point. This is arguably the best place in the park to scan for waterfowl. In addition to species previously mentioned, look in season for horned, eared, pied-billed, western, Clark's, and, on rare occasion, red-necked grebes. Check the nearby muddy peninsula to the south, in migration for yellowlegs, spotted, solitary, and least sandpipers, American pipit, and Wilson's snipe. American white pelican is abundant in summer.

The trail follows a row of trees along the shoreline to the northwest. In spring, migrants use these trees as a route around the lake. Check carefully! Almost anything can turn up here. Flocks of yellow-rumped warblers may have other species with them. On the left is brushy prairie, which is another place for towhees, blue grosbeak, Say's phoebe, and a variety of sparrows. Sagebrush sparrow has been found here on several occasions. Check the small lagoon on the right for waterfowl and great blue heron.

Keep right at the next two intersections and continue on the Cottonwood Trail as it passes through a thick stand of willows, crosses a small double footbridge, and again parallels Bear Creek. Watch and listen for the "peeyeer" call of western wood-pewee. Look also for black-headed grosbeak, black-capped chickadee, bushtit, warbling vireo, and great horned owl. Broad-winged hawk is sometimes seen in migration.

From here, our route joins a web of trails that all go, more or less, in the same westerly direction. It first joins the Redtail Trail; take a right here. Where part of the trail veers to the left, stay straight on the Redtail. At the next intersection, stay straight onto the Owl Trail. At this point, any of the trails will take you to our end point. Following the suggested route, at 7.0 miles, the trail passes the same footbridge over Bear Creek that we checked earlier from the north side. What the heck, check it again, but continue on the south side of the creek.

The trail is now in the floodplain of Bear Creek, with brushy hillside on the left, riparian woodland on the right, and a small lush valley in between. This is a fine place to find a migrating flycatcher, perhaps a lazuli bunting, lesser goldfinch, or a flock of cedar waxwings.

As you continue along the creek, it will soon reach the entrance road, and the loop closes. Cross the road to the Skunk Hollow parking lot.

The trail passes across a prairie area

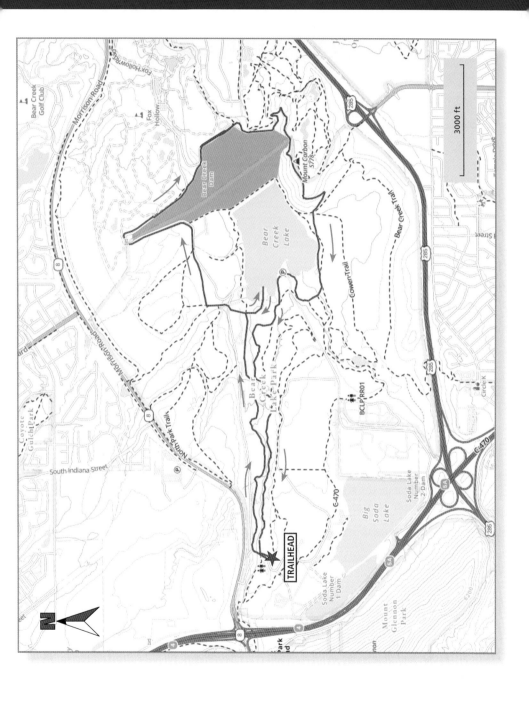

BEAR CREEK LAKE PARK

Chapter 19. **Chicago Lakes**

ROUND-TRIP DISTANCE	9.52 miles
ELEVATION GAIN	1,445 feet
MAX ELEVATION	11,776 feet
TRAIL TYPE	Out-and-back
DIFFICULTY	Strenuous
BEST SEASON(S)	Summer

FEATURED BIRDS: Yellow-rumped warbler, Cordilleran flycatcher, mountain chickadee, American robin, dark-eyed junco, red crossbill, red-naped sapsucker, Canadian jay, pine grosbeak, Clark's nutcracker, Wilson's warbler, Lincoln's sparrow, Barrow's goldeneye, mallard, spotted sandpiper, and great blue heron

COMMENT: This trail begins at the Echo Lake picnic area, at the opposite end of the lake from the lodge. It is the most strenuous of our hikes, due to a combination of length and elevation. It descends down the flank of a ridge, then climbs through a glaciated valley to the Chicago Lakes (upper and lower, though maps often do not refer to them as such). A glaciologist would classify these as "paternoster lakes," due to their resemblance to a string of religious beads. They occupy the upper end of the valley, near the "cirque" on the flank of Mount Evans, where the head of the glacier originated. The habitats the trail passes through include spruce-fir forest, creekside willow thickets, montane meadows, and above-treeline "tundra" at the end of the trail.

The hiker should be aware that the trail initially descends for one mile to Chicago Creek, and subsequently climbs for the remainder of the hike. This results in the same one-mile climb at the end of the hike with 374 feet of elevation gain, which can be a challenge at the end of a nine-mile round trip. I suggest taking a break with an energy snack before taking on the ascent at the end, which can be a hassle if you are tired. This hike includes a challenging bonus at the end of the trail!

Clark's nutcracker

Pine grosbeak

Signature species—Canada jay

GETTING THERE: From Denver take I-70 west for about twenty-five miles to Exit 240 at Idaho Springs. Turn south onto CO Highway 103 and follow it for twelve miles to Echo Lake Park.

THE ROUTE: The Chicago Lakes Trail hike begins at the stone picnic shelter at Echo Lake Park. Before leaving the area of the shelter, check the trees around the picnic area and the adjacent willow thickets. In midsummer, there will probably be several Cordilleran flycatchers giving their distinctive two-note call. Mountain chickadees are common, American robins are found in the conifers and on open ground, as are dark-eyed juncos (gray-headed race). In late summer, juvenile juncos may seem to be everywhere. Red crossbills are frequently seen here, and an occasional pine grosbeak makes an appearance. Red-naped sapsuckers work the trees, Canada jays patrol the picnic area in search of a snack to steal from an unwary picnicker, and the raucous calls of Clark's nutcrackers can be heard from the treetops. Look in the willows for Wilson's warbler and Lincoln's sparrow.

Follow the trail along the west end of Echo Lake and check the lake for the many resident mallards and Barrow's goldeneye. For several years Barrow's have nested here, and in summer are seen swimming about with ducklings in tow. Along the shore, look for spotted sandpiper and great blue heron. The rocky area just around the bend in the shoreline is a popular spot for several species of birds to drink and probe the sandy earth for invertebrates.

Brown-capped rosy-finch

Where the trail begins to loop around the lake, there is a junction. The trail to the left follows the lakeshore and eventually arrives at the lodge. Our route follows the trail to the right, which is well marked as the Chicago Lakes Trail and, after crossing a low ridge, begins the descent to Chicago Creek. This first section of the trail passes through spruce-fir woodland, and can be productive, especially if you happen upon a mixed-species feeding flock. Watch for downy and hairy woodpeckers; ruby-crowned and golden-crowned kinglets; pygmy, white-breasted, and red-breasted nuthatches; and many more of the typical higher-elevation coniferous forest species. American three-toed woodpecker is sometimes seen here.

The trail descends for a mile and a quarter to its low point at Chicago Creek, where a footbridge crosses the creek. Just beyond the bridge the trail joins a road and follows it for 0.9 mile. Along the way is Idaho Springs Reservoir, which, typical of lakes at this elevation, rarely has any waterfowl on it. Where the trail leaves the road, it becomes steeper and rockier, and in a quarter mile enters the Mount Evans Wilderness. Not long after entering the wilderness area you will begin to see a few standing dead trees and some occasional scorched deadfall. This is the lower edge of the burn area from the 1978 Reservoir Fire, which burned about 400 acres. Forests are slow to recover at these elevations, and the result is widely scattered live trees surrounded by meadow and the still-standing skeletons of the destroyed woodland. This habitat is suitable for a variety of species that prefer a more open

Bighorn sheep near the upper end of the valley

One of the Chicago Lakes

habitat to dense forest. In late summer, the area abounds with mountain bluebirds, including many hatch-year youngsters. Watch for Audubon's yellow-rumped warblers (yellow-throated, unlike the white-throated eastern type, Myrtle) flycatching from the dead snags, and Clark's nutcrackers screeching as they cruise up and down the valley. Check each bird using open perches among the dead trees; one of them is likely to be an olive-sided flycatcher. This is also a great vantage point from which to enjoy the views of the once-glaciated, ice-polished canyon walls gleaming in the sun and imagine what this valley might have looked like 10,000 years ago when it was filled with ice.

The trail continues to climb gradually, following Chicago Creek. There are sizable swaths of willow in this riparian corridor that are home to Wilson's warbler and Lincoln's and white-crowned sparrows. Check the brushy open woodlands for chipping sparrow and ruby-crowned kinglet.

At the 3.5-mile mark there is a creek crossing. Care should be exercised here, as the crossing requires some precarious rock-hopping. It is also another great place to check the willow thickets. White-crowned sparrows favor this area. Once across the creek, the trail continues the

Elephant head along the trail

Steller's jay

climb through open woodland until around 4.5 miles, where the lower of the two Chicago Lakes comes into view. The trail follows the side of the valley above the lake. Should you wish to visit the lake, there are a couple of spurs that provide access. From a birding perspective, there is little reason to do this, but sometimes we just find it necessary to stand on the banks of beautiful remnants of the glacial age.

Above the lake you will see an imposing cliff face crossing the valley. Ahead is the most strenuous part of the hike; the trail follows the right (west) side of the valley, climbing through a boulder field and gaining three hundred feet of elevation in a quarter mile. Be careful of steep slippery surfaces covered with fine grains of weathered granite. It would be an easy place to take a tumble.

As you gain the lip of the cliff and find yourself on flat ground, the upper of the Chicago Lakes lies before you, near the head of the valley and the cirque that birthed the glacier. Check the lake shores for American pipit. The remnant snowfields may have brown-capped rosy-finch, or the finches may appear with pipits by the lake. The scenery is its own reward. Spread out before you are the lake and the towering cliffs at the base of Mount Evans. Looking back the way you came, you will have a magnificent view back down the valley of Chicago Creek. It is a worthy payoff for the effort it took to get here. There are many rocks around the area, which make a fine seat to have a snack and enjoy your marvelous surroundings.

BONUS: Here is the bonus, if you want to call it that. Our route officially ends here, but for the strong of heart and leg, one last challenge remains. The trail that crosses the valley makes a steep ascent up the valley wall, rising over a thousand feet in little more than a half mile. The terminus is at Summit Lake, a cirque lake at the foot of Mount Evans. The rewards for completing this climb include the possibilities of seeing rosy-finches and pipits at the lake and, with a bit of luck, white-tailed ptarmigan on the surrounding tundra. Mountain goats and bighorn sheep are also seen in the area.

Since the trail extension ends at the Summit Lake parking area, this is an opportunity to leave one car at a parking lot, if you choose to take on the steep ascent. Or, you can just do the hike up to the upper Chicago Lake and then drive up to see Summit Lake and Mounts Evans later. In any case, as you work your way back down the trail, keep your eyes and ears on the alert for any species that you may have missed on the way up while executing this hike!

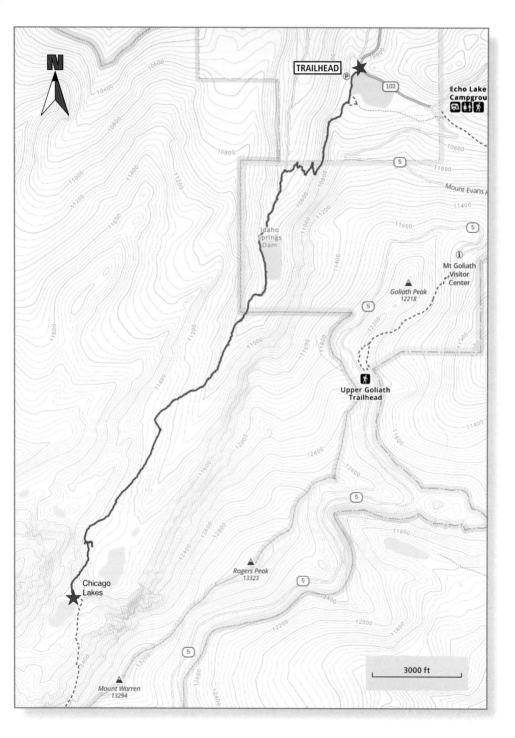

CHICAGO LAKES

Chapter 20. Mount Falcon Park

ROUND-TRIP DISTANCE	3.6 miles
ELEVATION GAIN	Parmalee Trail: 682 feet; Tower Trail: 334 feet
MAX ELEVATION	7,842 feet
TRAIL TYPE	Loop
DIFFICULTY	Moderate
BEST SEASON(S)	Summer

FEATURED BIRDS: One of Colorado's most sought-after birds, dusky grouse can sometimes be seen here. Other birds include spotted and green-tailed towhee; red crossbill (dependent upon quality of cone crop); pygmy, white-breasted, and red-breasted nuthatches; mountain and western bluebirds; Townsend's solitaire; Virginia's, yellow-rumped, and yellow warblers; black-capped and mountain chickadees; hairy woodpecker; and mixed flocks of winter finches

COMMENT: Mount Falcon is one of many Jefferson County Parks and Open Space properties. It features a variety of habitats, but most of the park consists of mountain meadow and coniferous forest.

The park is of historic as well as biological interest. John Brisben Walker, who was instrumental in the establishment of Red Rocks Park, owned the property that is now Mount Falcon in the early twentieth century. He and his wife, Ethel, began construction of a hilltop castle in 1909. He envisioned the home as a western White House, which would be used by presidents as a summer home, named Walker's Dream. The castle was completed, but Ethel passed away in 1916 and the castle burned down in 1918. All that remains is a rock skeleton. It can be reached via the Castle Trail.

Mount Falcon is crisscrossed by a web of trails. The route described provides good birding opportunities and can be broken into two

Dusky grouse

Hairy woodpecker

parts: Parmalee Trail and Tower Trail. Please note that the lower parts of the Castle Trail, as well as the Turkey Trot Trail, can be accessed from the East Trailhead in Morrison, and have opportunities for hillside scrub specialist species like both towhees and Woodhouse's scrub-jay.

GETTING THERE: From C-470, take the Morrison exit. Proceed west up Bear Creek Canyon for approximately 8.5 miles to Kittridge. From Kittridge, take Myers Gulch road south (left) for 2.7 miles to Picutis. Turn left and follow the signs to Mount Falcon Park.

Mount Falcon Park can also be accessed from Highway 285, taking the Indian Hills exit and driving 2.5 miles to Picutis. Alternate trails, not described here, can be accessed at the Mount Falcon East Trailhead, located off CO Highway 8 south of Morrison.

THE ROUTE: Our hike will begin at the upper parking lot. Proceed down the main trail and stop at the kiosk for a map. In the winter, this stretch of trail can see mixed-species flocks, and is accessible except during heavy snowfall. After stopping at the kiosk, take the first right turn onto Parmalee Trail. Check the brush along the first hundred yards of the trail for towhees, and the adjacent meadow for bluebirds, chipping sparrows, the gray-headed form of dark-eyed junco, soaring

The Parmalee Trail drops into the valley

ravens, red-tailed hawks, and hairy woodpecker. After a couple hundred yards, the trail drops steeply through Douglas fir, juniper, and ponderosa. Look for Townsend's solitaires on the junipers and woodpeckers in the pines. The rest of the route may provide all three nuthatches, western tanager, pine siskin, and a variety of other coniferous specialties.

As the trail begins to flatten a bit (although this part of the trail is rarely flat), watch the open woodlands for dusky grouse. These birds may be seen feeding on the ground, but may also perch in trees. Their cryptic coloration can make them difficult to spot.

The trail passes several low points and drainages along the way, which can be good for moist-habitat birds like hermit thrush, MacGillivray's warbler, and Lincoln's sparrow. The trail then begins to ascend up its sunnier, southeast-facing section. Here the open brushy slopes are preferred by towhees, bluebirds, black-headed grosbeak, blue-gray gnatcatcher, and bushtit. Eventually you will come to the intersection of the Parmalee, Meadow, and Tower Trails. After scanning the meadow for mountain blue-birds, take a sharp left and follow the Tower Trail to the top of Mount Falcon, where you can visit an observation tower. Sometimes rock wren can be seen in the boulders near the base of the platform. Continuing along the Tower Trail, you will soon reach the Eagle Eye Shelter. The shelter commands fine views of Mount Evans to the west and the valley below. Around the shelter is another place to see towhees, chipping sparrow, dark-eyed junco, and rock wren.

A short distance farther will bring you to the Meadow Trail, which follows the edge of the largest meadow in the park. Look for bluebirds and other meadow specialists. The Meadow Trail then intersects with the Castle Trail again. Take a left turn, which will allow you to follow the margin of a large burn scar from a 1980s fire. Until the dead trees began to lose their bark, this was a go-to location for American three-toed woodpecker. These birds can still occasionally be seen in the area. Our route ends where the Castle Trail meets the Parmalee Trail and the loop closes.

Mount Falcon lookout tower

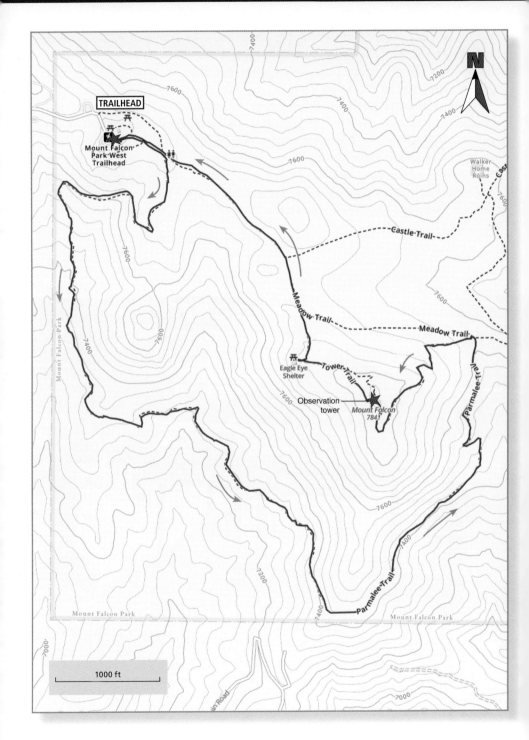

MOUNT FALCON PARK

Chapter 21. **Silver Dollar Lake**

ROUND-TRIP DISTANCE	6 miles
ELEVATION GAIN	1,466 feet
MAX ELEVATION	12,201 feet
TRAIL TYPE	Out-and-back
DIFFICULTY	Moderate to strenuous
BEST SEASON(S)	Summer

FEATURED BIRDS: Mountain chickadee, all three nuthatches, pine grosbeak, hairy and American three-toed woodpecker, dark-eyed junco, dusky grouse, northern goshawk, yellow-rumped (Audubon's race) and Wilson's warblers, white-crowned sparrow, Lincoln's sparrow, fox sparrow, American pipit, white-tailed ptarmigan, brown-capped rosy-finch, golden eagle, and pine grosbeak

COMMENT: The Silver Dollar Lake Trail is a mixed-habitat hike. It begins in spruce-fir forest and climbs to above-treeline tundra with two montane lakes. The first two-mile section is a moderate hike that climbs gradually and passes through forest, past some rock glaciers, onto the tundra, and brings you to Silver Dollar Lake. The last half mile is a strenuous climb with elevation gain equaling the first section of the trail.

GETTING THERE: Take I-70 west of Denver to Exit 228 at Georgetown. Exit toward Georgetown and you will immediately come to a roundabout. Make a right turn onto Argentine Street and follow it as it continues straight and turns into Brownell Street. At the T-intersection with 6th Street, turn left toward downtown Georgetown and go two blocks to Rose Street. From 6th and Rose, it is 8.6 miles to the turnoff at a parking lot. Turn right on Rose and go four blocks to its intersection with Guanella Pass Road. Turn left on Guanella Pass Road and follow

Hiking through the thickets above tree line

it for 8.4 miles to the parking lot on the right. You can begin the trail here to add some elevation, but if you prefer to save some walking, follow the road for 0.6 mile up to the second parking lot. This is the Silver Dollar Lakes Trailhead.

THE ROUTE: Beginning at the upper parking lot, the trail at first climbs through spruce-fir forest with two creek crossings. This part of the hike is good for many species typical of spruce-fir habitat. Watch and listen for mountain chickadee, ruby-crowned and golden-crowned kinglets, hermit thrush, red crossbill, Steller's and Canada jays, pine siskin, and the raucous Clark's nutcrackers. Listen for the quiet pecking of hairy and American three-toed woodpeckers. Northern goshawk has been seen here, though this species is scarce and typically hard to find. In the open areas within the forest, listen for olive-sided flycatchers giving their calls for malted beverages, "Quick! Three beers!" Dusky grouse is possible here too.

Pine grosbeak

The trail descends along the glaciated valley

At the 0.8-mile mark, you will come upon an impressive rock glacier on the left. These massive rock fields are moving slowly down the mountainside through the process of frost heaving, whereby the rocks are lifted slightly by winter freezing and lowered a bit by the spring thaw. This rock glacier usually has several pikas scampering among the boulders. Listen for their squeaky calls. Pika are being forced steadily to higher elevations by climate change.

Not long after you have passed the rock glacier, the trees begin to dwindle and a lake comes into view on the right. This is Naylor Lake, and while it contributes to the scenery, it is private and off-limits to hikers. As you pass Naylor Lake, the trail continues to climb past the last of the forest and onto the open alpine tundra. The habitat here is a mix of grassland and willow thicket. Although the willows may initially seem to be lifeless, stay alert! They are actually teeming with birdlife, most of which manage to remain unseen. If you stop, listen, and watch you will

Yellow-bellied marmot

eventually see a few of the little rascals popping up to have a look around. Watch for a flash of brilliant yellow as a Wilson's warbler flits through the bushes, and listen for the distinctive song of a fox sparrow. White-crowned sparrows (the black-lored mountain race) will perch on high twigs, but are just as often seen crossing the trail while working the ground for bugs and seeds. Lincoln's sparrows, with their beautiful but cryptic plumage, also skulk in these thickets, but will periodically choose a high perch from which to survey their territory.

Even into late summer there may be remnant snowfields on the north-facing south valley walls. Check these for the brown-capped rosy-finches that like to pick insects off the surface of the snow.

At the 1.8-mile mark is Silver Dollar Lake. As with most high-elevation lakes, Silver Dollar is barren of birdlife. It is worthwhile to check the shoreline for a spotted sandpiper or American pipit. The pipits tend to stick to rocky, wet habitats as they make their winter descent from the alpine tundra to the lowlands, where they can be found along gravel bars in creeks and rivers.

Up to this point, the hike has been moderate with a gradual ascent to Silver Dollar Lake. Above the lake, it becomes more strenuous, with a rapid half-mile ascent to Murray Lake up a steep, rocky stretch of trail. Fortunately, the scenery from this vantage point creates an excuse for frequent stops to catch your breath. Remember to make note of the wildflowers; the steep slopes along this part of the trail can be covered with brilliant Indian paintbrush in late summer. Many other wildflowers and high-elevation butterflies can also be found here, so take a little time to enhance your birding by checking out some of the other benefits of this route.

American pipit by the upper lake

Steller's jay

Silver Dollar Lake

At 2.25 miles, the trail tops a low rise, which is the maximum elevation on the trail. A short walk down the other side brings you to Murray Lake, which is much like Silver Dollar Lake below. Check the shore for pipits or you may see a golden eagle riding the updrafts from the valley walls high above. Be sure to check the tiny valley carved by the drainage from the lake. It abounds with wildflowers and butterflies, and some of the bird specialties of alpine habitat may be seen taking advantage of the abundance of food and shelter near the stream.

The hike finishes with a return via the same route you took on the way up. A relaxed downhill walk should provide plenty of opportunity to take your time and observe some of the features that you might have missed on the way up!

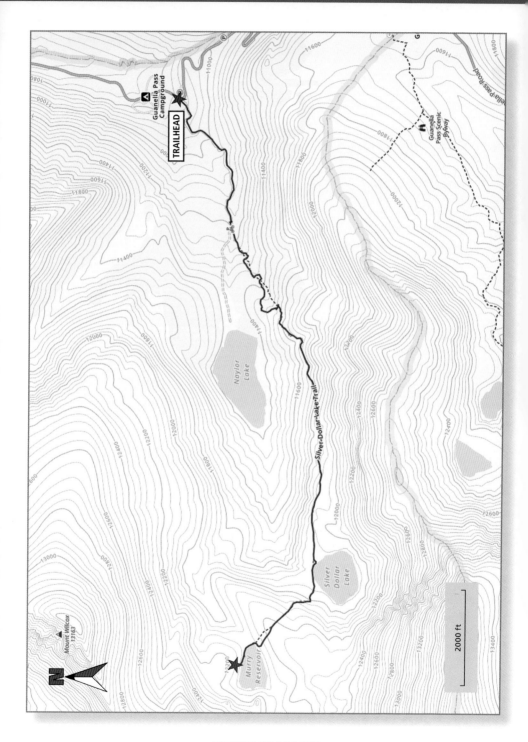

SILVER DOLLAR LAKE

Chapter 22. **Flying J Ranch**

ROUND-TRIP DISTANCE	3.3 miles
ELEVATION GAIN	514 feet
MAX ELEVATION	8,263 feet
TRAIL TYPE	Loop
DIFFICULTY	Easy
BEST SEASON(S)	Summer

FEATURED BIRDS: American three-toed woodpecker; red crossbill; pygmy, white-breasted, and red-breasted nuthatches; red-naped and Williamson's sapsuckers; and most of the foothills/montane species

COMMENT: Flying J is a Jefferson County Open Space park. This trail is perfect for the hiker who would like to do some miles, see a variety of montane birds, and spend quality mountain time without a lot of elevation gain. The park has become a known site for American three-toed woodpecker. It can also be good for wildflowers in season.

In recent years there has been considerable forest management at Flying J, as hundreds of dead trees have been felled, stacked, or shredded. In many areas, this activity has created new open areas littered with wood chips, which may look a little odd but can be fine areas for species that prefer open woodlands, like bluebirds, some flycatchers, and Townsend's solitaire. The park has restrooms and picnic shelters.

GETTING THERE: Follow C-470 from either the north or south to the Highway 285 exit. Take 285 for eleven miles toward Conifer to the Barkley Road exit. Take the exit, then turn left, and in a half mile, turn right on County Road 73. Follow 73 for 0.7 mile to the park entrance. Continue to the parking lot, which is the trailhead.

THE ROUTE: The route follows the Shadow Pine Trail/Loop all the way around the park. For purposes of this

Western tanager

Brown creeper

Signature species—red crossbill

book, we will proceed counterclockwise, though either direction works well. Begin at the parking lot and check the pines here first. Many montane species have been found in this immediate area. There are almost always red crossbills in the area. Then follow the Shadow Pine Trail west into the mixed coniferous forest. With a few exceptions, the habitat is mostly uniform forest and typical mid-elevation birds can be found throughout. There are sizable tracts of lodgepole pine along the way, which tend to be "biological deserts," so it is best to move along and spend more time among the spruce, fir, and ponderosa pine, where ruby-crowned and golden-crowned kinglets, brown creeper, downy and hairy woodpeckers, Cordilleran fly-catcher, yellow-rumped warbler (Audubon's), and all three nuthatches are usually present in numbers in summer.

Open woodland habitat, typical of much of the trail

At 0.8 mile from the trailhead, there is an open meadow area from which dead and dying trees have been removed. As of this writing, there are large piles of logs on either side of the trail. Here is a good site to spend a little time. The log piles are magnets for American three-toed woodpeckers, which have become something of a specialty of the park. Look for flying bark as the woodpecker flings it in all directions while searching for delectables living just under the surface.

Mountain bluebird, common in open meadow habitat

The meadow is prime habitat for birds that prefer more open spaces, such as western wood-pewee, dark-eyed junco (gray-headed form: the only race that breeds in Colorado), mountain and western bluebirds, and broad-tailed and rufous hummingbirds. Here (as well as other open spaces that provide views of treetops) is a good opportunity to look for Townsend's solitaire and red crossbill, birds that have the cooperative habit of perching at the very tops of trees. This is also a good area to scan the skies for red-tailed hawk, turkey vulture, and some of the more unusual raptors. Feeling lucky? Perhaps a northern goshawk will zip by!

In another mile and a quarter, the trail intersects a drainage, where you will find a bench that makes a fine place to rest and watch for passing birds. Between the moist thickets in the drainage and the adjacent forest, there is plenty of potential for good variety. Look for Wilson's and MacGillivray's warblers, Lincoln's sparrow, house wren, and common yellowthroat. The marshy area straddling the trail has a variety of wildflowers, and this is the best place in the park to find butterflies, though they aren't abundant here.

The rest of the trail has repetitive habitat, as would be expected of a route with little elevation gain. Mountain chickadees and violet-green swallows are ubiquitous and abundant, and black-capped chickadee, olive-sided flycatcher, spotted and green-tailed towhees, and western tanager may also be present. The last quarter mile of the loop can be productive; many birds like the open mixed woodland of this cleared area. In spring, look for Williamson's sapsucker inspecting prospective nest cavities, bluebirds and yellow-rumped warblers hunting from open perches, and mixed flocks of swallows filling the skies overhead.

Upon completing the loop, you may want to check the pond to the north of the parking area. While not included on our loop, it provides an opportunity to see waterfowl and some of the water-centric birds, like common yellowthroat and several species of swallows.

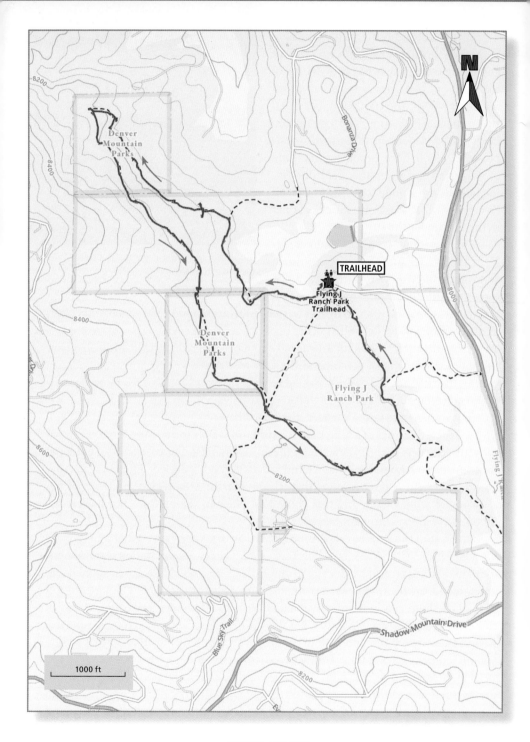

FLYING J RANCH

Chapter 23. **Staunton State Park**

ROUND-TRIP DISTANCE	Davis Ponds: 2.15 miles; Mason Creek: 7 miles
ELEVATION GAIN	Davis Ponds: 329 feet; Mason Creek: 1,229 feet
MAX ELEVATION	9,419 feet
TRAIL TYPE	Loop
DIFFICULTY	Easy (Davis Ponds) to moderate (Mason Creek)
BEST SEASON(S)	Summer

FEATURED BIRDS: Red-naped and Williamson's sapsuckers; hairy and downy woodpeckers; mountain and black-capped chickadees; plumbeous and warbling vireos; western bluebird; white-breasted, red-breasted, and pygmy nuthatches; Steller's jay; green-tailed and spotted towhees; violet-green, barn, and tree swallows; ruby-crowned kinglet; olive-sided flycatcher; white-throated swift; canyon and rock wrens; hermit thrush; Clark's nutcracker; golden-crowned kinglet; dark-eyed junco (gray-headed race); Canada jay; peregrine falcon; northern goshawk; and dusky grouse

COMMENT: Staunton is one of Colorado's newest state parks. It includes a variety of habitats, including coniferous and aspen woodlands, mountain prairie, creek riparian, and towering cliffs. This is a fee area.

Our hike here includes two parts which can be done in tandem or individually. The Davis Ponds loop is shorter and with less elevation gain than the Mason Creek loop. Davis Ponds includes tracts of prairie, open woodland, moist drainages, and aspen groves, while Mason Creek (actually a combination of the Mason Creek, Old Mill, and Staunton Ranch Trails) has more homogenous habitat of mostly coniferous forest at the foot of impressive cliffs. Although the Davis Ponds loop doesn't wander far from the 8,200-foot contour, the Mason Creek loop climbs to just above 9,400 feet and brings the hiker in close proximity to the Staunton Rocks, which are popular among climbers. The combination of additional elevation and cliff habitat does add a few additional species to the mix.

An osprey waits patiently at Davis Ponds

Staunton Rocks

GETTING THERE: Take Highway 285 west from C-470 for nineteen miles to Shaffers Crossing. Exit and go north (right) on Elk Creek Road for 1.7 miles to the park entrance.

THE ROUTE: The Davis Ponds Trail begins at the parking area that is adjacent to the group picnic pavilion. You will stay on the Davis Ponds Trail for the entire hike. As you start down the trail you will come to the junction that will eventually close the Davis Ponds loop. For our route, stay to the right and shortly you will enter a wide prairie area. This area is good for species that prefer meadows and open woodlands, such as western bluebird, Townsend's solitaire, western wood-pewee, Empidonax flycatchers (Staunton has least, Hammond's, dusky, and Cordilleran), and various woodpeckers. Continue walking through the meadow/open woodland habitat that characterizes this part of the park, passing the junction with the Chase Meadow Trail.

At just over a half mile there is a spur to the left that serves as a cutoff between two sections of the Davis Ponds Trail. Stay to the right on the main trail and soon the trail will turn to the southwest and follow Black Mountain Creek, which feeds the ponds. The aspens in this area are riddled with woodpecker cavities, which makes it a good area to find cavity nesters. Red-naped sapsucker, pygmy nuthatch, and western bluebird are usually easy to see here.

Follow the trail down to the ponds, where two footbridges will enable you to circle around. There will usually be a few barn, tree, and violet-green swallows around the ponds, but the ponds do not attract much in the way of waterfowl. There might be a mallard or the occasional great blue heron. A specialty in summer is osprey, which may be seen swooping down from a treetop to catch a fish.

Cross the second bridge and return to the Davis Ponds Trail to walk through open woodland. Pay particular attention to the areas near the ponds, as they tend to have great bird density. Many additional species can be seen here, including olive-sided flycatcher, brown creeper, Canada and Steller's jays, plumbeous vireo, and ruby-crowned kinglet. American three-toed woodpecker and northern goshawk are rare but regular. In late summer, yellow-rumped warblers abound.

Olive-sided flycatcher

Follow the Davis Ponds Trail back to the trailhead, passing the cutoff that connects with the northern part of the trail (unless you want to see some additional open woodland).

The Mason Creek loop begins at the same parking area and meanders to the east, where it begins to follow, appropriately enough, Mason Creek. The trail ascends rapidly for a mile, passing through ever-denser coniferous forest along the creek. Listen here for the haunting song of the hermit thrush.

At about 2.4 miles the Bear Paw Trail cuts off to the left. While this side trail climbs up to a couple of nice overlooks, it doesn't add anything to the birding, so our route continues up the Mason Creek Trail for another two miles to the ruins of the old mill. This is the topmost portion of our hike and along this stretch is a good place to watch for some of the higher-elevation species, like Canada jay, Clark's nutcracker, and golden-crowned kinglet. As you approach the impressive cliff faces of the Staunton Rocks, watch and listen for rock and canyon wren. Look high above for silhouettes of white-throated swifts darting past the towering rocks. Peregrine falcon is possible here.

Our descent will follow the Old Mill Trail, which roughly parallels Black Mountain Creek but does not intersect with it. If you should choose to continue west on the Border Line and Bugling Elk Trails, many more miles of trail become available, as well as access to Elk Falls and the Elk Falls Overlook.

After about a mile, the Old Mill Trail intersects both the Staunton Ranch Trail and South Upper Ranch Road. Either will take you back to the parking area, with the road being a bit more direct and the trail passing through extra open woodland habitat, where you have additional opportunities to see species you may have missed in the park.

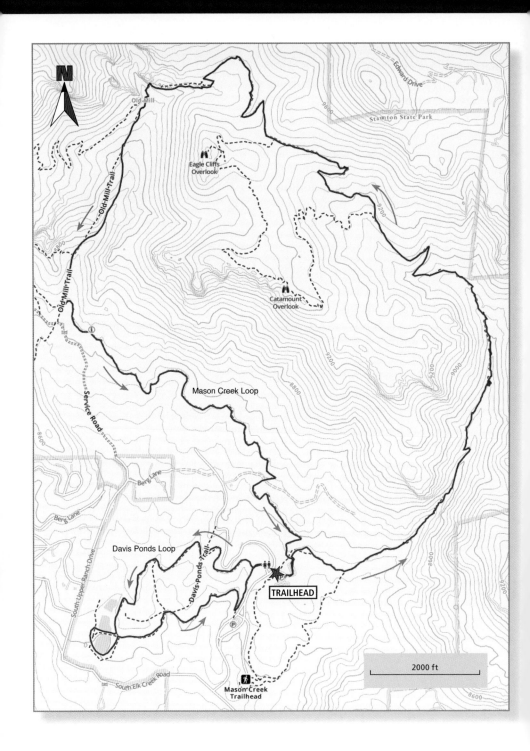

STAUNTON STATE PARK

Chapter 24. **Waterton Canyon**

ROUND-TRIP DISTANCE	13 miles
ELEVATION GAIN	550 feet
MAX ELEVATION	5,807 feet
TRAIL TYPE	Out-and-back
DIFFICULTY	Moderate
BEST SEASON(S)	All

FEATURED BIRDS: Gray catbird, lazuli bunting, yellow-breasted chat, canyon wren, green-tailed and spotted towhees, all six Colorado swallows, lesser goldfinch, song sparrow, warbling vireo, bushtit, Bullock's oriole, white-throated swift, and Cordilleran flycatcher

COMMENT: Waterton Canyon is managed by Denver Water in partnership with the US Forest Service. Be sure to check the applicable rules before birding here. The area is subject to occasional closures for maintenance. The trail is actually a road (closed to public traffic) that follows the South Platte River and runs from Waterton Road to the Strontia Dam area. Consequently, the walking conditions here are excellent. The only departure from the road is the short stretch of trail that splits from the road and passes through a small brushy woodland to the south. The entire route has good birding, but some of the best is along this part of the trail, as this is the only deciduous woodland on the hike.

Waterton Canyon is also the first leg of The Colorado Trail. Note that there is a resident herd of bighorn sheep in Waterton Canyon. Should you be lucky enough to encounter the sheep, please enjoy them while keeping your distance. Human contact can stress this declining species, and, being wild, their behavior can be unpredictable.

GETTING THERE: Take C-470 east or west to Wadsworth Boulevard. Exit and go south for about 4.5 miles to Waterton

Cordilleran flycatcher

The overhead pipes that divide the upper and lower parts of the canyon

Road. At Waterton Road you must turn left. After turning left, you will pass the Audubon Center on the left and in another 300 yards, the Waterton Canyon parking lot on the left. Walk west from the parking lot, cross Waterton Road, and you will be at the trailhead for Waterton Canyon.

THE ROUTE: From the trailhead, the road (hereafter referred to as the trail) passes some buildings and soon runs along some brushy rock outcrops. This is great habitat for both towhees, as well as lesser goldfinch, bushtit, and an occasional rock wren. Bullock's orioles also like this habitat, as well as the woodland ahead, where they nest.

Spotted towhee

At the 0.4-mile mark, an obvious trail splits to the south (left) from the main trail and passes through brushy woodland. Look for yellow-breasted chats, which are frequently found in the large bushes. Listen for their bizarre mix of whistles, toots, cackles, and trills. Western wood-pewee is common here, and warbling vireos nest in the cottonwoods. There are also opportunities to view the river. Black phoebe has been recorded here. Watch and listen for the flight rattles of belted kingfishers plying the river for unwary fish. Common mergansers are often on the river, especially in winter.

Sharing the trail with the bighorns

This short trail rejoins the main trail at about 0.8 mile, leaving the woodland and running between the river on the south and brushy slopes to the north. This is one of the best areas to find the lazuli bunting and lesser goldfinch. In the thickets along the river are gray catbird and yellow warbler. Look in the brush on the hillsides for spotted and green-tailed towhees. Many of the birds of this area also like to perch on the utility lines on the north side of the road.

At 1.25 miles, you will reach the overhead pipes, which is a dividing point for the canyon. (For *eBird* users, the canyon is divided into "from Waterton Road to overhead pipes" and "upstream of overhead pipes.") The area around the pipes is excellent for swallows; bank is unusual here, but cliff, violet-green, tree, barn, and northern rough-wing are all usually present. The trail beyond the pipes is bighorn sheep territory. They usually do not venture closer to the mouth of the canyon than this, but are often seen in the next several miles, upstream of the pipes.

The next few miles feature towering rock faces and pine woodland on the south and a mix of small copses of trees and rocky ledges on the north. Watch the ledges for nesting Cordilleran flycatcher and listen for the descending song of the canyon wren. As the trail gains a little elevation, chances for more montane species increase. Hairy woodpecker, western tanager, pygmy nuthatch, mountain and western bluebirds, Townsend's solitaire, and MacGillvray's warbler may be found here, while birds of the foothills scrub continue. Keep an eye out for Say's phoebe and Woodhouse's scrub-jay.

At about 3.5 miles there is the Marston Diversion Dam, which has a small impoundment behind it. This lake is not too productive, but look in summer for common merganser and common goldeneye in winter. Continuing upstream, look for the stiff-winged flight of white-throated swifts working the cliff faces for flying prey.

From this point to the end of the outward-bound portion of the hike, the habitat is uniform and hosts a mix of foothill and montane species. Other birds to look for include golden and bald eagles, red-tailed hawk, ruby-crowned and golden-crowned kinglets, pine siskin, and yellow-rumped warbler.

The end of our route is marked by the junction of Waterton Canyon and Colorado Trails. From here there are good views of the Strontia Springs Dam (closed to the public), and there is a shelter, which is a great place to take a break and have lunch before retracing the route back to Waterton Road. Or, of course, you can continue up The Colorado Trail for a few hundred miles, but time and equipment constraints will probably dictate the former strategy.

Bighorn sheep

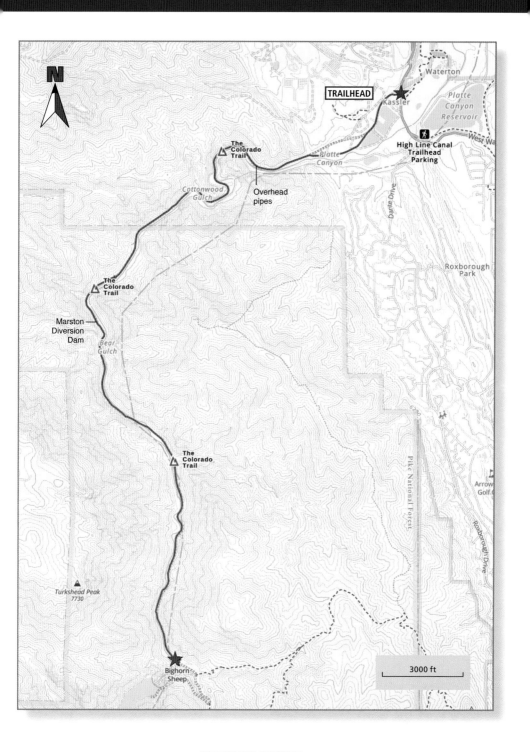

WATERTON CANYON

Chapter 25. **Roxborough State Park**

ROUND-TRIP DISTANCE	8.4 miles
ELEVATION GAIN	1,626 feet
MAX ELEVATION	7,169 feet
TRAIL TYPE	Loop or out-and-back
DIFFICULTY	Moderate
BEST SEASON(S)	Summer

FEATURED BIRDS: Spotted towhee, green-tailed towhee, lazuli bunting, blue-gray gnatcatcher, canyon wren, Woodhouse's scrub-jay, Virginia's warbler, black-headed grosbeak, plumbeous vireo, Steller's jay, warbling vireo, and hermit thrush

COMMENT: Roxborough State Park is a landscape of striking scenic beauty, comprising uptilted red rock formations of the same type as found in the famous Red Rocks Park. The park does not feature a variety of habitats but is a superb example of foothills scrub habitat and its birds. As the trail ascends, it affords great views of the park and at the higher elevations, the park and the eastern plains beyond. This is a fee area.

GETTING THERE: From C-470, take the Wadsworth exit and drive 4.3 miles south to the intersection with Waterton Road (this is just before the Lockheed Martin gate). Go left on Waterton Road and continue as the road winds around to the east for 1.5 miles to the intersection with Rampart Range Road. Go right (south) on Rampart Range for 2.1 miles to Roxborough Park Road, and take a left. In about a quarter of a mile, take a right on Roxborough Park Drive and continue into the park.

Green-tailed towhee

THE ROUTE: This route begins at the visitor center. Proceed across the parking lot to the west, where the Carpenter Peak/Elk Valley Trailhead can be found. As you start up this trail, you will pass through grassy prairies surrounded by large tracts of brushy habitat. Here you should find

The Fountain Formation flatirons from the high point

Woodhouse's scrub-jay, blue-gray gnatcatcher, and black-headed grosbeak. In areas of scrubby trees and brush, look for lazuli buntings perched and Virgina's warblers skulking in the understory.

A little over two miles up the trail is the junction of Carpenter Peak and Elk Valley Trails. We will bear right on the Carpenter Peak Trail, but will emerge later on the Elk Valley Trail as we complete our loop. From this point the trail begins to climb a bit more steeply and soon conifers begin to appear. As the pines and spruce-fir become more numerous and develop into small thickets, listen for the raspy question-and-answer song of plumbeous vireo and the rapid up-and-down cadence of warbling vireo. Broad-tailed hummingbirds can be abundant here too. Listen for the ethereal song of the hermit thrush where the woods become thick and moist.

Upon reaching the top of Carpenter Peak, the colorful formations of the park, as well as the vast expanse of the eastern plains, are laid out before you. It is a vista that is worth spending a little time with.

At the bottom of the short drop down from the peak is the junction of the Carpenter Peak and Powerline Trails. If you are at all pressed for time, return by the same route we have just described. For our purposes, the descent will be down the

The forested valley between flatirons

Powerline Trail, much of which follows the clear-cut for the lines. This will add an additional mile to the hike, and allows for the inclusion of some new territory to bird. Along the power line clearance area is a lot of second-growth brush and small trees, and the birds that may be seen here are much the same as on the hike up.

Just before the Powerline Trail reaches Iron Bark Drive, you will come to the junction with the Elk Valley Trail. Take this trail to the left (north). It will wind across gentle brushy slopes that are habitat for lazuli bunting, lesser goldfinch, and spotted towhee, which at times seem to be everywhere. Follow the Elk Valley Trail back to its junction with the Carpenter Peak Trail, and return via the previous route to the visitor center.

Black-headed grosbeak

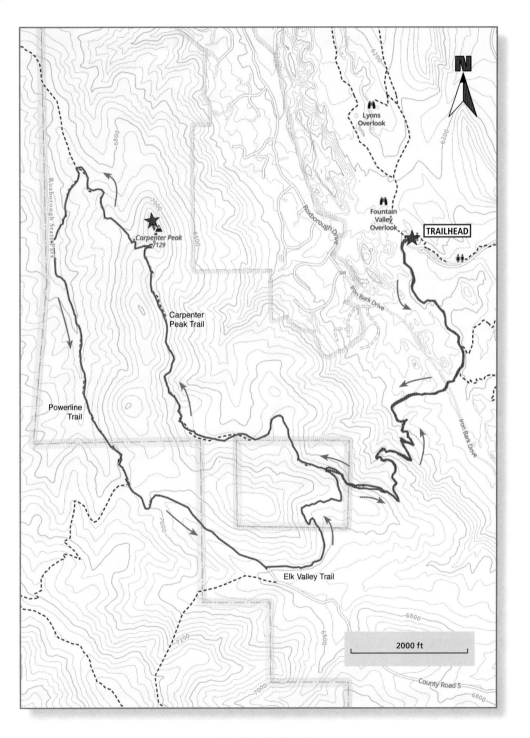

ROXBOROUGH STATE PARK

Chapter 26. Rampart Range

ROUND-TRIP DISTANCE	1.7 miles
ELEVATION GAIN	368 feet
MAX ELEVATION	7,640 feet
TRAIL TYPE	Loop or out-and-back
DIFFICULTY	Easy
BEST SEASON(S)	All

FEATURED BIRDS: Williamson's and red-naped sapsuckers; American three-toed woodpecker; broad-tailed hummingbird; western wood-pewee; olive-sided flycatcher; willow, least, dusky, Hammond's, and Cordilleran flycatchers (the Empids); ruby-crowned kinglet; plumbeous and warbling vireos; yellow-rumped and Mac-Gillivray's warblers; hermit thrush; lesser goldfinch; green-tailed towhee; chipping sparrow; dark-eyed junco (gray-headed); red crossbill; Cassin's finch; pine grosbeak; evening grosbeak; pine siskin; Townsend's solitaire; northern pygmy-owl; hairy and downy woodpecker; northern flicker; white-breasted, red-breasted, and pygmy nuthatches; Steller's jay; mountain and black-capped chickadees; and brown creeper

COMMENT: The Rampart Range hike is the most informal of our hikes; there is no maintained or named trail here. It is more of a route than a trail, but it is also one of our best for foothills montane species. It is monocultural in that there is no habitat variety—the hike is within ponderosa forest with some spruce-fir included.

There is little understory, which makes the area ideal for observing ground specialists like juncos and towhees, and also makes it easy to do a little wandering and observing. At times, bird density here is impressive. In May, the birdsong can be almost deafening at times. Since there is so little habitat diversity, I will not make attempts to describe possible sightings at specific locations along the trail, but rather have included many of the possibilities in the Featured Birds section. Be aware that all of these are possible anywhere along the route.

Evening grosbeak

Trail through mixed coniferous woodland

Boulder field looking south toward Pikes Peak

NOTE: The parking lot that serves this hike is also heavily used by ATV and dirt bike riders. The ORV trail starts at the same place as our trail but quickly deviates from our route, so there is little interference. However, expect possible noise at the trailhead. While birding in this area can be excellent in winter, there is likely to be snow and ice. Please plan accordingly. Restrooms are available but not well maintained.

GETTING THERE: From the north, take C-470 to Highway 85 (Santa Fe Drive). From the south, take Highway 85 north from Castle Rock. At Sedalia, take Highway 67 west for ten miles to its intersection with Rampart Range Road. Go left (south) to the parking lot, which will then be on your immediate right.

Juvenile and male red crossbills

THE ROUTE: The trail leaves the parking lot at the southwest corner and enters ponderosa forest. The stretch of trail from the parking lot to the first intersection, about 200 yards, often has some of the best birding. Watch and listen for seasonal birds. Here and all along the trail, watch the treetops for perching red crossbills (this is, in my opinion, the best place to see crossbills in the whole region) and Cassin's finches. At the intersection, turn right and proceed down a slight grade. Check the aspen grove below on the right and listen (especially in spring) for the arrhythmic jazz drumming of red-naped sapsuckers. This open woodland area often has multiple olive-sided flycatchers loudly demanding, "Quick! Three beers!" Check the brushy areas for green-tailed and spotted towhees.

Continue around the bend to the left, following the ridge until you reach a boulder field. A short detour to your right will bring you to a vantage point among the boulders, which furnishes an opportunity to look down upon some of the adjacent forest and views to the south toward Pikes Peak. Ruby-crowned kinglets are abundant in this area.

At this point our hike calls for some off-trail bushwhacking, though there are few bushes to contend with. Drop into the small valley to the left (east) and continue up the far side, where you will find another trail. If you have chosen the loop option, turn left and follow the trail back to the parking lot. This, however, makes for a very short hike. Instead, turn right and follow the trail through open woodland to its end, which is marked by two wooden posts. This will not provide any change of habitat, but provides a chance for more of the featured species. The posts are the boundary with private property. Turn around and retrace your steps back to the north, passing the point where you reentered this trail from the valley and continuing to the trailhead at the parking lot.

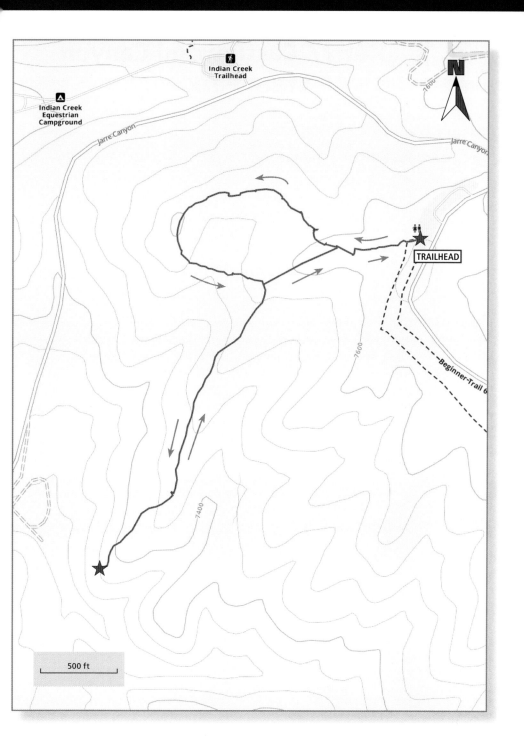

RAMPART RANGE

Chapter 27. Castlewood Canyon State Park

ROUND-TRIP DISTANCE	3.75 miles
ELEVATION GAIN	560 feet
MAX ELEVATION	6,400 feet
TRAIL TYPE	Loop/Figure-eight
DIFFICULTY	Easy
BEST SEASON(S)	Early summer

FEATURED BIRDS: Broad-tailed hummingbird; hairy woodpecker; Cordilleran flycatcher; plumbeous vireo; Steller's jay; common raven; mountain chickadee; red-breasted and pygmy nuthatches; ovenbird; red crossbill; pine siskin; western tanager; turkey vulture; white-throated swift; warbling vireo (red-eyed vireo is seen here occasionally); several corvids (black-billed magpie, Woodhouse's scrub-jay, blue jay, American crow, and common raven); swallows; bushtit; blue-gray gnatcatcher; rock, house, and canyon wrens; western and mountain bluebirds; Townsend's solitaire; lesser goldfinch; chipping, lark, vesper, and song sparrows; green-tailed and spotted towhees; dark-eyed junco; yellow-breasted chat; bobolink; western meadowlark; Bullock's oriole; red-winged blackbird; Virginia's, yellow, and yellow-rumped warblers; black-headed and blue grosbeaks; and lazuli bunting

A signature winter bird—Townsend's solitaire

COMMENT: The small canyon of Castlewood was formed by the continued erosive action of Cherry Creek. The park is situated in the northernmost part of the Black Forest. The Black Forest (also known as the Palmer Divide) is an ecological outlier of the Rocky Mountain foothills, which extends out into the plains and abuts the prairie. As such, it hosts many species normally found in the mountains. The park is also of significant geological and historical

The author near the old breached dam

interest. The ruin of the 1890s Lucas Homestead can be seen in the north part of the park. The south part of the park features the old Castlewood Dam, which collapsed in 1933 and caused catastrophic flooding in Denver. The remnants of the dam can be seen on this hike.

The geology of the park is simple but interesting. The lowest layer, found along the floor of the canyon (and exposed by the scouring action of the 1933 flood), is the Dawson Arkose. This material was laid down 55 million years ago when the area was a swamp. Above the Dawson is the Wall Mountain Tuff, a rhyolitic (light-colored lava and volcanic ash and debris) volcanic rock that was blasted onto the area 36.7 million years ago by a huge eruption near present-day Salida. The top layer, which forms the rim of the canyon, is the Castle Rock Conglomerate. Many gigantic boulders of this formation have fallen from the cliffs and come to rest in the bottom of the canyon. Check the boulders for the variety of pebbles and cobbles contained within the conglomerate. These originated up in the Rockies and were worn smooth

The canyon

Arid rocky upland habitat

by the action of the continental streams, which carried them here and deposited them in the sand and silt, which would later solidify into the conglomerate.

The state park contains several distinct habitats, including ponderosa savannah (also known as foothills ponderosa), oak scrub (composed primarily of Gambel oak), caprock, grassland (prairie), and riparian. Our hike will take us through or near each of these, as well as one bonus habitat: valley grassland/agricultural. While not within the park boundary, this habitat can be viewed from several points along our route.

GETTING THERE: From north or south take I-25 to Exit 184/Founders Parkway. Follow Founders Parkway (Highway 86) east for 5.6 miles to Fifth Street (Highway 86). Turn left (east) on Highway 86 for 5.9 miles to Franktown. At Franktown, turn right (south) on Highway 83 for 4.9 miles to the park entrance.

NOTE: The entrance to Castlewood Canyon State Park north can be found on the south side of Highway 86 west of Franktown, and just west of the bridge over Cherry Creek.

THE ROUTE: Our hike begins and ends at the visitor center. Before you begin the hike, take a look around the visitor center area. The center has a video that relates the history of the dam disaster. The vegetation surrounding the center frequently has green-tailed and spotted towhees, house finches, dark-eyed juncos of several races (winter), house finches, and possibly a Woodhouse's scrub-jay.

Walk north from the center and across the adjacent parking lot to the beginning of the Canyon View Nature Trail. This paved trail wanders along the rim and provides views of the inner canyon, including overlooks at 0.15 and 0.35 mile along the way. Listen for the song of the canyon wren and watch the skies for raptors. Red-

Heavily vegetated inner canyon

tailed hawks are frequently seen soaring. In the colder months, Townsend's solitaires winter in the park in numbers. Since they make a cooperative habit of sitting at the tops of pines and their favorite tree, the juniper, they are easy to see. A recent winter hike here turned up more than twenty solitaires. The open ponderosa woodland/scrub habitat is suitable for many other species, including all three nuthatches, downy woodpecker, lark sparrow, and blue grosbeak.

At the 0.7-mile mark, you will reach the intersection of the K (Inner Canyon) and L (Lake Gulch) Trails. Either trail will work, but for our purposes, take the L Trail and proceed up a slight grade to the nearby Canyon Point parking lot. At the parking lot, continue on the paved trail to the right, which soon becomes unpaved and begins a descent down the southwest-facing slope of the ridge. For the next mile you will pass through ponderosa woodland and oak-scrub-covered slopes that are a fine place to see bushtit, eastern and western kingbirds, blue-gray gnatcatcher, black-headed grosbeak, Virginia's warbler, green-tailed and spotted towhees, and yellow-breasted chat.

Along this stretch of trail are several overlooks that give views of the valley below. This valley, known colloquially among birders as "Winkler Ranch," is a combination of grassland and hayfields. In early summer you can see nesting bobolinks rising out of the vegetation and occasionally perching in plain view. Red-winged

The trail crosses the creek through willow thicket habitat

blackbirds also nest here. Along the road on the far side of the valley are many bluebird nest boxes, which are shared by western and mountain bluebirds and tree swallows. If time permits after your hike, return to the entrance to the north section of the park (just west of Franktown) and take the drive through the park. This road will eventually exit the park and follow the valley to the south, providing good looks at the nesting bluebirds and swallows, and additional opportunities to see the bobolinks.

At the 1.7-mile mark, we reach the creek at the bottom of the canyon. Use the designated rocks to cross the creek. On the other side is the L and K Trails intersection and a spur extending to the west. Follow this spur a short distance to have a look at the old Castlewood Dam. The spur also serves as the connector between the trails of the north and south sections of the park. Follow it to the north to connect with the north trails, if that is your plan. However, our route takes us back to the intersection, where we pick up the K (Inner Canyon) Trail.

Here things change dramatically. The Inner Canyon Trail, as the name suggests, follows the lower section of the canyon back to the southeast along Cherry Creek. We leave the upland habitats of the L Trail and work through riparian vegetation and some pine-oak along the way. Note that this trail passes through, among, and over some sizable boulders, so it should not be attempted by anyone with mobility issues. On the plus side, the trail is mostly shaded and there are benches along the way where you can take a break on a warm summer day.

Watch and listen along the creek for song sparrow and common yellowthroat in the riparian thickets. Gray catbird can also be found here, and warbling vireos nest

The visitor center

in the trees. The pine trees scattered along the trail, as well as the denser forest on the southwest wall, provide great opportunities to see many of the Black Forest specialties, including plumbeous vireo, Steller's jay, mountain chickadee, red crossbill, pine siskin, and western tanager. Check moist ledges for nesting sites of Cordilleran flycatcher.

The habitat is uniform for the next three-quarters of a mile, as the trail winds along the creek. At the end of this stretch there is a bridge across the creek, and the trail climbs steeply back to the rim. This section along the canyon wall is heavily forested and is a good place to look for both chickadees, downy and hairy woodpecker, northern flicker, American robin, and most of the Black Forest specialties.

At the top of the climb up the canyon wall, the Inner Canyon Trail meets the Lake Gulch Trail at the spot where we earlier made a left turn and walked up to the Canyon Point parking lot. This closes the top loop of the figure eight. If you wish, you can retrace your steps along the canyon rim and back to the visitor center. However, our route will take us back up to the parking lot and the 3.25-mile mark of our hike. From here, we will turn left rather than right, and follow the road for the last half mile back to the visitor center. The road follows the boundary between the ponderosa savannah and the adjacent prairie, and gives us an opportunity to add a few more species to our list. In the open areas among the pines and oak scrub, watch for blue jay, western wood-pewee, lark and chipping sparrows, lesser goldfinch, yellow and yellow-rumped warblers, and Bullock's oriole.

As you walk the road, you will have views of the open prairie to your right. Watch the fence line and the grasslands beyond for specialties of that habitat, including Say's phoebe, western meadowlark, both kingbirds, vesper sparrow, blue grosbeak, and lazuli bunting.

The road takes you back to the visitor center, where you can take a break, watch the movie, have a few adventures in retail, and reminisce about your completed hiking/birding adventure.

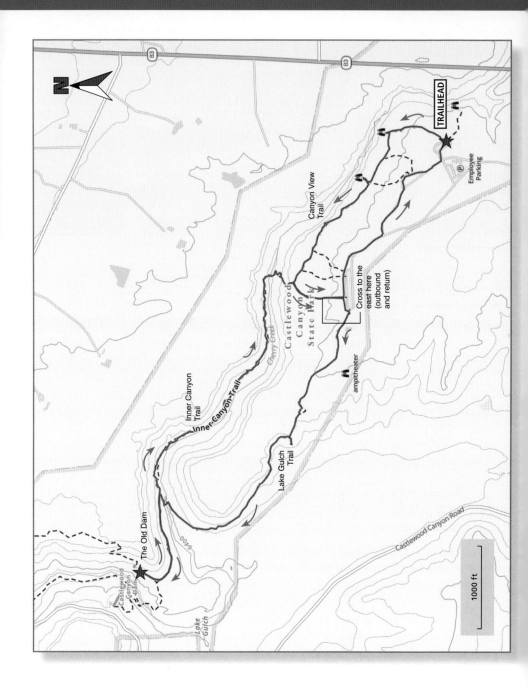

CASTLEWOOD CANYON STATE PARK

Chapter 28. **Red Rock Canyon Park**

ROUND-TRIP DISTANCE	6.1 miles
ELEVATION GAIN	1,468 feet
MAX ELEVATION	6,701 feet
TRAIL TYPE	Loop
DIFFICULTY	Moderate
BEST SEASON(S)	Summer and winter

FEATURED BIRDS: Black-chinned hummingbird, western wood-pewee, Say's phoebe, black-capped chickadee, plumbeous and warbling vireos, blue-gray gnat-catcher, lesser goldfinch, band-tailed pigeon, white-throated swift, Virginia's warbler, black-headed grosbeak, northern shrike, Steller's jay, mountain chickadee, Townsend's solitaire, Cassin's finch, pine siskin, dark-eyed junco, white-crowned sparrow, downy woodpecker, Woodhouse's scrub-jay, bushtit, white-breasted nuthatch, American goldfinch, and song sparrow

COMMENT: Red Rock Canyon is a Colorado Springs city park, encompassing 1,474 acres of foothills ridge and valley terrain. As its name suggests, the park is similar in geology and topography to other parks along the Front Range, including Red Rocks, Roxborough, and Garden of the Gods. Its unique landscape makes this park attractive to birders: a combination of scrub-oak-covered ridges, grassy meadows, ponderosa forest in the valleys, rocky cliffs, with tracts of pinyon-juniper scattered among the other habitats.

GETTING THERE: Take I-25 in Colorado Springs from either direction to the Cimarron Street exit. Go west on Cimarron/Highway 24 for three miles to the signed entrance to the park. Turn left (south) on Ridge Road, enter the roundabout, and take the second exit into the park. Pass the first parking lot and continue for a quarter mile to the second parking lot. This is the trailhead for our hike.

Western wood-pewee

The trail passes through the Quarry

THE ROUTE: As with many of our hikes, the chosen route is only one of many possibilities. Our hike is straightforward in that it consists of several traverses across ridges and valleys.

It begins at the designated parking lot at the Red Rock Canyon Trailhead. As you follow this trail, begin looking for typical birds of arid uplands, such as black-billed magpie, canyon towhee, and rock wren. Also keep in mind that Red Rock Canyon has all four of the commonly occurring hummingbirds in Colorado: broad-tailed and black-chinned in summer, and calliope and rufous in fall migration. Follow the trail for 0.7 mile to its intersection with the Quarry Trail, and follow it to the right as it climbs the first ridge. You will soon arrive at the Quarry, where red rock from the Fountain Formation was removed for use in constructing several buildings in Colorado Springs.

Here the trail becomes the Quarry Pass Trail, as it passes through the notch in the ridge created by quarry operations. Continue to follow this trail for 0.45 mile, as it crosses the Greenlee Trail and winds through tracts of Gambel oak to a hairpin turn. Here there is a good view of Pikes Peak. While walking through the many tracts of scrub oak, watch for the specialties of this habitat, including Woodhouse's scrub-jay and bushtit (all year), northern shrike, mountain chickadee, white-crowned sparrow (winter) and blue-gray gnatcatcher, band-tailed pigeon, green-tailed towhee, Virginia's warbler, and black-headed grosbeak (summer). Watch also for spotted towhee, which is common in summer with a few remaining all year.

After rounding the corner there is an intersection with the Mesa Trail, which our route follows southwest along a scrub-covered ridge and crosses the Roundup Trail. Watch for all the previously referenced species as well as northern shrike (winter). In 0.8 mile from the Pikes Peak view, the trail attains its maximum elevation of 6,700 feet and turns sharply to the east. Continue on the Mesa Trail for 0.4 mile to where it again intersects the Roundup Trail, which you will then follow as it descends into the adjacent canyon. In this area there are numerous junipers, the preferred winter habitat of Townsend's solitaires that have left their summer home in the mountains for the lower elevations of the foothills. In summer, check the cliffs along the north side of the trail for white-throated swifts and listen for canyon wren.

This canyon supports the best stand of ponderosa pine (and other conifers) in the park. There is an opportunity to see a number of species that don't appear in other habitats in the park. Look in the conifers for plumbeous and warbling vireos (summer); ruby-crowned and golden-crowned kinglets (winter); black-capped

Ridges rise above the forested canyons

Woodhouse's scrub-jay

(all year); mountain chickadees (winter); white-breasted, red-breasted, and pygmy nuthatches (all year); pine siskin and Cassin's finch (winter); Steller's jay (winter); and western tanager (summer). If you are hiking in winter, use caution in the canyon bottom as the trail there is frequently icy and/or muddy, and can be hazardous.

The trail emerges from the canyon and turns to the northeast. In two hundred yards there is an intersection of the Red Rock Canyon Trail and an unnamed spur. Follow the spur to the right (east), past a pond, which at this writing is being backfilled with rock, and into the valley meadow beyond. In the valley, watch for black-billed magpie, western bluebird (early spring to summer), and Say's phoebe (summer). At the east side of the valley, the cross trail ends in a T where the Lion and Landfill Trails meet. Either will work for our purposes, but the Lion Trail offers great views of the quarry before making a hairpin turn and climbing south up the ridge. Large stands of scrub oak are found here, which host the same suite of birds as described earlier.

At the end of the ridge there is an intersection of several trails, including the Lion, Upper Codell, 26th Street, and Landfill Trails. This is the second-highest elevation along our route at 6,660 feet. For an extra workout, take the Upper Codell Trail. Our route, however, will follow the 26th Street Trail south and then around a sharp bend to the left and back around to the northeast. In 0.3 mile, the 26th Street Connection drops off to the right and our trail merges with the Hogback Valley Trail.

In another 0.3 mile, the Codell and Lower Codell Trails branch off to the right. All three of these trails reconnect a

Spotted towhee

little farther along, but the best choice is the Codell Trail, which follows the eastern-most ridge in the park and provides views of the valley and ridge to the west and of the city to the east. In 0.75 mile, the Codell Trail rejoins the Hogback Valley Trail. Along this stretch, scan the skies for raptors and watch the valley for Say's phoebe and western kingbird (summer). Shortly after returning to the Hogback Valley Trail, you will reach the intersection with the Red Rock Rim Trail, which then ascends a shallow slope and meets the Upper and Lower Hogback Trails. The rocky outcrop-pings along this stretch can produce canyon (all year) and rock (summer) wrens and canyon and spotted towhees (all year).

From here, take either the Upper or Lower Hogback Trail around the meadow in the shallow bowl below a low ridge and look for a spur off the main trail that drops sharply to our ending point back at the parking lot.

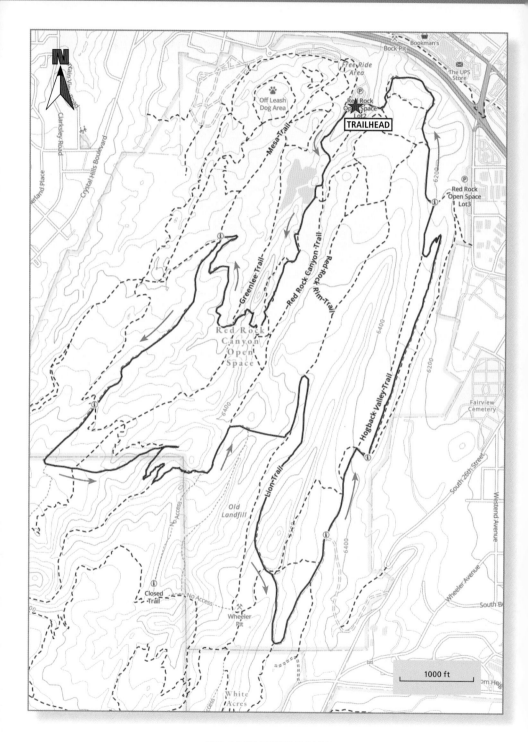

RED ROCK CANYON PARK

Chapter 29. **Cheyenne Mountain State Park**

ROUND-TRIP DISTANCE	6.6 miles
ELEVATION GAIN	1,500 feet
MAX ELEVATION	6,719 feet
TRAIL TYPE	Double loop
DIFFICULTY	Moderate
BEST SEASON(S)	Summer

FEATURED BIRDS: Wild turkey; Woodhouse's scrub-jay; blue-gray gnatcatcher; spotted towhee; bushtit; yellow-breasted chat; Virginia's warbler; ash-throated flycatcher; Say's phoebe; western kingbird; black-headed grosbeak; blue grosbeak; lazuli bunting; black-chinned hummingbird; black-capped and mountain chickadees; plumbeous vireo; white-breasted, red-breasted, and pygmy nuthatches; pine siskin; ovenbird; Townsend's solitaire; hermit thrush; western wood-pewee; dusky, Hammond's, and olive-sided flycatchers; ruby-crowed kinglet; broad-tailed hummingbird; red-tailed hawk; golden eagle; and white-throated swift

COMMENT: This is a fee area. Cheyenne Mountain is a state park and has excellent facilities, including a good array of camping sites. It features numerous trails; a trail

Fort Carson

Cheyenne Mountain

map is available at the visitor center. As with many parks, the trails are heavily used by mountain bikers and the hiker must stay aware.

GETTING THERE: From I-25 in Colorado Springs, take Exit 140 to Highway 115. Go south on CO 115 about seven miles to the entrance to Cheyenne Mountain State Park. Turn right on JL Ranch Heights Road, pass the roundabout, and stop at the visitor center for a map. A quarter mile down the road there is a left turn that leads to a large parking lot, information kiosk, restrooms, and the Limekiln Trailhead.

Fall color in the oak scrub

THE ROUTE: This hike is somewhat unique in that it is bimodal; it begins in scrub habitat and tops out in mixed deciduous forest, with no other habitats present. The species encountered in each mode will include those described in the Featured Birds section. There are no lakes or marshes; hence, no waterfowl are to be expected. The descent does not follow the same track as the ascent, but passes through the same habitat zones, so species encountered on the way down will be the same as those seen on the way up.

After beginning on the Zook Loop, our hike will follow the Sundance and Talon Trails. Begin at the information kiosk adjacent to the parking lot and take the Zook Loop to the west. At 0.15 mile, stay right on the Zook Loop, and in another quarter mile, go left on the Sundance Loop. Follow the Sundance Loop past the intersection with the Little Bear Trail.

At the half-mile mark, follow the Sundance as it makes a sharp right. Do not go straight on the Turkey Trot Trail, unless you wish to return to the parking lot. Gambel oak scrub is the dominant habitat for the next mile. Watch for black-chinned hummingbird, Woodhouse's scrub-jay, wild turkey, and spotted towhee. Listen for the unique toots and whistles of yellow-breasted chat. Virginia's warbler nests here, and this is also a habitat for bushtit and blue-gray gnatcatcher. There are areas of prairie among the widespread thickets of scrub. In these open areas

The trail passes through oak scrub

Virginia's warbler

look for low-elevation flycatchers, like Say's phoebe, ash-throated flycatcher, and western and eastern kingbird. Such areas are also a fine place to look for birds from the cardinal family, including black-headed and blue grosbeaks and lazuli bunting. Check buntings carefully; indigo bunting is sometimes seen here. Mountain and western bluebirds also frequent this habitat.

As the trail slowly gains elevation, the habitat begins to change a little. Ponderosa pines begin to appear among the brush, mountain mahogany joins the Gambel oak in the scrub, and some pinyon-juniper appears. Cheyenne Mountain is not known for pinyon-juniper species—although an occasional pinyon jay or juniper titmouse might appear, don't count on it. For these species, try the Aiken Canyon hike a few miles to the south, where pinyon-juniper is the dominant habitat. On the other hand, this transition zone is a good place to look for open woodland species like lesser goldfinch, western wood-pewee, ruby-crowned kinglet, and white-breasted nuthatch. You can also watch and listen in early summer for ovenbird, which nests here, though you are more likely to encounter one a little higher up. When passing through open areas, scan Cheyenne Mountain itself; you might see white-throated swifts flitting across its face.

At 1.5 miles is the intersection with the Talon Trail. Go right (left for a shorter hike) to continue the route. Ponderosa begins to dominate the landscape and spruce-fir appears. At this point, black-capped and mountain chickadees are common and red-breasted and pygmy nuthatch enter the mix. At 2.4 miles, there is a short spur to the right that leads to an overlook. Have a look if you wish, but there is no shortage of fine views along the trail. This area is also good for the coniferous forest flycatcher group: Hammond's, dusky, and olive-sided. Listen for the "Quick! Three beers!" of the olive-sided flycatcher. Broad-tailed hummingbirds are common in summer. Rufous hummingbird is sometimes seen in fall migration.

At 2.55 miles, pass the intersection with the North Talon Trail (a perfectly good alternative with similar habitat) to intersect with the South Talon Trail in 0.3 mile. There is a bench, which is a great place to take a break and listen for the ethereal song of the hermit thrush. After resting for a bit, take the left turn onto the South Talon, and begin a 1-mile (almost) loop that continues through mixed coniferous forest and reaches the high point of the hike. Along the way, you may encounter pine siskin or Cassin's finch, or perhaps hear the hoarse question-and-answer song of plumbeous vireo. Townsend's solitaire sings its rollicking song in summer, but switches to lonely toots as it moves downslope in the fall.

At 3.9 miles, the South Talon rejoins the Talon Trail, and the descent begins. Scan the sky occasionally for red-tailed hawk or even a golden eagle. At 5.3 miles, the Talon and Sundance Trails merge, and then split a few yards farther along. Go left on Talon and shortly you are back in scrub oak. As you continue, you will encounter the intersections with the ends of the Turkey Trot and Little Bear Trails, whose opposite ends you passed on the way up. Along the way are nest boxes. Check for bluebirds and tree swallow in spring.

At 6.5 miles, the loop closes as the Talon Trail rejoins the Zook Loop. Cross the bridge (check for sparrows along the ditch) and continue straight to the parking lot or take the small detour to the right on the Sundance Trail for a bit more habitat.

Canyon towhee

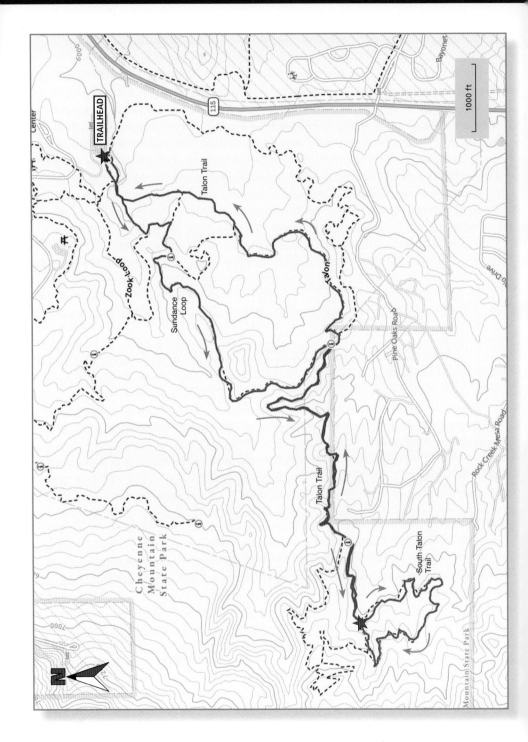

CHEYENNE MOUNTAIN STATE PARK

Chapter 30. Aiken Canyon Preserve

ROUND-TRIP DISTANCE	3.4 miles
ELEVATION GAIN	519 feet
MAX ELEVATION	6,868 feet
TRAIL TYPE	Loop
DIFFICULTY	Easy to moderate
BEST SEASON(S)	Spring and summer

FEATURED BIRDS: Juniper titmouse, bushtit, pinyon jay, Woodhouse's scrub-jay, Bewick's wren, Say's phoebe, cedar waxwing, and western bluebird

COMMENT: The Aiken Canyon Preserve is a state property managed by The Nature Conservancy. It is a fine example of pinyon-juniper habitat, and that is the primary reason it is included here. The trail offers an opportunity to see many of the pinyon-juniper specialties that are scarce elsewhere. Continued development is threatening this type of foothills habitat along the Front Range, making this 1,621-acre property especially valuable.

Juniper titmouse

Bewick's wren

GETTING THERE: From I-25 in Colorado Springs, take Highway 115 for 14 miles toward Cañon City. Turn right on Turkey Canyon Ranch Road, and the parking lot for the visitor kiosk and trailhead will be on the right.

THE ROUTE: Our hike begins at the visitor kiosk. For birding purposes, do not neglect this area. There are frequently a number of species found right around the parking lot and kiosk. The trail starts off to the east, passing through open grassland and along a usually dry creek bed. In this open area, look for Say's phoebe, western bluebird, sage thrasher, and lark sparrow. Check for scaled quail in brushy areas. Ash-throated flycatcher is sometimes seen here.

At the 0.7-mile mark, the trail splits and the loop begins. Bear right, and as the elevation increases a bit, pinyon-juniper forest dominates. This hike is a bit of a one-trick pony in terms of habitat. Birds to be found here include pinyon jay, juniper titmouse, bushtit, and Bewick's wren.

Green-tailed (migration) and spotted (all seasons) towhees are fairly common in brushy areas. Blue-gray gnatcatcher (summer) and black-throated gray warbler (migration) are also found, as well as western tanager and black-headed grosbeak (summer). Look in all seasons for black-capped and mountain chickadees. Cordille-

Pinyon jay

Western bluebird

Mountain bluebird

ran flycatcher, western wood-pewee, lazuli bunting, and Virginia's warbler are here in summer, and dusky flycatcher in migration.

About halfway around the loop, two spurs depart from the main trail. Taking the right (north) spur will lead you into Aiken Canyon, through dense coniferous woodlands, and eventually it ends at some cabin ruins. We will not include that trail here, as we have plenty of coniferous forest birding opportunities at other locations. However, it is a scenic and potentially rewarding side route, so it is worth a look if you are so inclined. In the area around this intersection, look for white-breasted, red-breasted, and pygmy nuthatches (all seasons); lesser goldfinch (summer); and golden-crowned kinglet and Townsend's solitaire (winter).

The left (south) spur takes you up a short scramble to the top of the hill that this loop encircles. Again, it is worth taking this short side climb if only for the view.

Beyond the two optional spurs, the main trail gradually descends through more pinyon-juniper habitat and, eventually, brushy grassland. In addition to the pinyon-juniper specialties, look for cedar waxwing, warbling and plumbeous vireos, black-chinned hummingbird (summer), and MacGillivray's warbler (migration) to round out your list.

Soon the trail reaches the split where we began our loop, and the return follows the same route we took earlier.

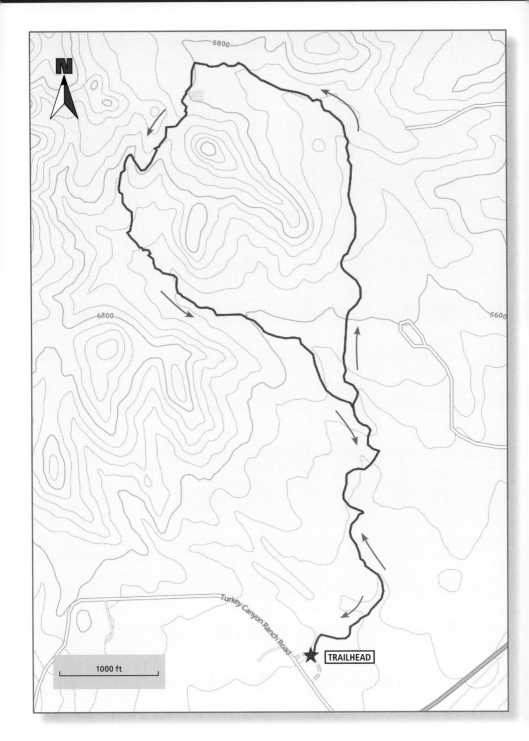

AIKEN CANYON PRESERVE

CODE OF BIRDING ETHICS

Courtesy of the American Birding Association

Practice and promote respectful, enjoyable, and thoughtful birding as defined in this code.

1. Respect and promote birds and their environment.

(a) Support the conservation of birds and their habitats. Engage in and promote bird-friendly practices whenever possible, such as keeping cats and other domestic animals indoors or controlled, acting to prevent window strikes, maintaining safe feeding stations, landscaping with native plants, drinking shade-grown coffee, and advocating for conservation policies. Be mindful of any negative environmental impacts of your activities, including contributing to climate change. Reduce or offset such impacts as much as you are able.

(b) Avoid stressing birds or exposing them to danger. Be particularly cautious around active nests and nesting colonies, roosts, display sites, and feeding sites. Limit the use of recordings and other audio methods of attracting birds, particularly in heavily birded areas, for species that are rare in the area, and for species that are threatened or endangered. Always exercise caution and restraint when photographing, recording, or otherwise approaching birds.

(c) Always minimize habitat disturbance. Consider the benefits of staying on trails, preserving snags, and similar practices.

2. Respect and promote the birding community and its individual members.

(a) Be an exemplary ethical role model by following this Code and leading by example. Always bird and report with honesty and integrity.

(b) Respect the interests, rights, and skill levels of fellow birders, as well as people participating in other outdoor activities. Freely share your knowledge and experience and be especially helpful to beginning birders.

(c) Share bird observations freely, provided such reporting would not violate other sections of this Code, as birders, ornithologists, and conservationists derive considerable benefit from publicly available bird sightings.

(d) Approach instances of perceived unethical birding behavior with sensitivity and respect; try to resolve the matter in a positive manner, keeping in mind that perspectives vary. Use the situation as an opportunity to teach by example and to introduce more people to this Code.

(e) In group birding situations, promote knowledge by everyone in the group of the practices in this Code and ensure that the group does not unduly interfere with others using the same area.

3. Respect and promote the law and the rights of others.

(a) Never enter private property without the landowner's permission. Respect the interests of and interact positively with people living in the area where you are birding.

(b) Familiarize yourself with and follow all laws, rules, and regulations governing activities at your birding location. In particular, be aware of regulations related to birds, such as disturbance of protected nesting areas or sensitive habitats, and the use of audio or food lures.

Birding should be fun and help build a better future for birds, for birders, and for all people.

Birds and birding opportunities are shared resources that should be open and accessible to all.

Birders should always give back more than they take.

SPECIES OF SPECIAL INTEREST

In completing some of these trails, the hiker is encouraged to observe and enjoy as many birds as possible. However, there will inevitably be certain species of special interest to an individual, and it would be helpful to be able to determine where they might be found. The following list is intended to be helpful in that regard. It is not intended to be comprehensive. The listings here will represent one or more ideal location(s) for a given species, which may occur on other routes. The species that are included as special interest reflect my opinion. I have tried to create a complete list of interesting birds that may occur on our hikes, excluding common species (American robin, European starling, black-billed magpie, etc.) that might be seen almost anywhere.

The birds are listed in current taxonomic order, so they should parallel the listings in your field guide, depending upon the age of the guide and how often species have been shuffled since it was published. The locations are indicated by chapter number and comments are added where appropriate. If a trail is particularly favorable for the species, the number will appear in boldface. These designations are from my own experience and are strictly anecdotal.

Wood duck	9, 12
Dabbling ducks (including blue-winged and cinnamon teal, northern shoveler, gadwall, American wigeon, mallard, northern pintail, and green-winged teal)	**9**, 12, **13**
Diving ducks (including canvasback, redhead, ring-necked duck, greater and lesser scaup, bufflehead, common goldeneye, hooded, common and red-breasted merganser, and ruddy duck)	**9, 12**, 13
Barrow's goldeneye	**10**
Ring-necked pheasant	9
White-tailed ptarmigan	7, 19 (particularly at Summit Lake if the final very steep optional climb is added)
Dusky grouse	1, 4, 5, 15, 19, 20, 21, 22, 26 (In spite of the multiple locations, the grouse is hard to find anywhere.)
Wild turkey	**4, 5**
Pied-billed grebe	**9**, 10, **12, 13**, 14, 18
Horned and eared grebes	**9, 12**
Western and Clark's grebes	**9**, 12, 18
Band-tailed pigeon	1, 2, 15, 19, 20, 21, 22, 26, 29 (This unpredictable species can be found anywhere in the mountains, but nowhere with any regularity.)
Black swift	6 (If present, they will be around the falls.)
White-throated swift	**3, 16**, 23, **24**, 28, 29
Black-chinned hummingbird	**13**, 28, 29
Broad-tailed hummingbird	1, 4, **11, 15, 17**, 19, 20, 21, 22, 23, 29
Virginia rail	12, 13
Sora	12, 13
Plovers (including black-bellied and semipalmated, killdeer)	**9**, 10, **12**, 13, 14, 18
Long-billed curlew	9, 12 (A prairie specialist; only a few of our hikes have the proper habitat, and even at these locations sighting a curlew would be unusual.)
Sandpipers (including marbled godwit; sanderling; long-billed dowitcher; lesser and greater yellowlegs; Wilson's and red-necked phalaropes; and Baird's, least, semipalmated, and western sandpipers)	**9** (by far the best, especially in fall migration), 12, 13, 18

Spotted sandpiper	**9**, 10, 13, **14**, 18
Sabine's gull	**9**, 12 (usually found only around large bodies of water in migration)
Gulls (including Bonaparte's, Franklin's, ring-billed, California, herring, Iceland, and lesser black-backed)	**9** (by far the best), 12, 18
Black tern	**9**, 12
Terns (including common and Forster's)	**9**, 12, 18
Loons (including red-throated, Pacific, and common)	**9** (winter)
Double-crested cormorant	**9**, 10, **12**, **13**, **18**
Great blue heron, great and snowy egret	**9**, 10, 12, **13**, 14, **18**
Bald eagle	**9**, **12** (especially in winter)
Northern harrier	9, 12
Hawks (including Swainson's, red-tailed, and rough-legged)	2, **9**, **12**, 18
Barn owl	9 (check nest boxes)
Great horned owl	9, 12, 14, 16, **18** (This magnificent bird can be found on any of our hikes with open deciduous woodlands, especially lower elevations with black-billed magpies, as the owls frequently utilize their nests. Great horned owls do not build, they remodel!)
Northern pygmy-owl	16, 17 (These are two localities where this bird has been found in winter; they are irregular and there are no "high probability" sites.)
Burrowing owl	**11** (There are also multiple prairie dog colonies around the arsenal that can be checked after completing the hike, especially at the northwest corner of the refuge.)
Northern saw-whet owl	1, 4, 5, 15, 17, 19, 20, 21, 22, 23, 26 (Do not be misled by the number of localities; this species is common in the foothills but hard to find.)
Belted kingfisher	**9**, 10, 13, **14**, 17, 18, 24
Sapsuckers (including Williamson's and red-naped)	1, 4, 5, **15**, 19, 20, 21, **22**, **23**, **26** (look in mixed pine-aspen habitat)
American three-toed woodpecker	1, 15, **19**, 20, 21, **22**, 23, **26** (coniferous forest, especially with recently dead trees)
Peregrine falcon	2, 3, **16**, 24, 25, 28, 29 (anywhere with cliffs)

Prairie falcon	9, 12, **16, 25,** 29 (true to its name, prefers prairie but nests on cliffs)
Olive-sided flycatcher	1, 4, 5, 15, 19, 20, **22, 23, 26,** 29
Hammond's flycatcher	same as olive-sided flycatcher
Dusky flycatcher	same as olive-sided flycatcher
Cordilleran flycatcher	**3,** 11, **17,** 23, **24** (lower-elevation foothills, forests, and canyons near water)
Shrikes (including loggerhead in summer and northern in winter)	**2, 9, 12,** 16, 27, 28
Plumbeous vireo	**1,** 4, 5, **8,** 11, **15, 17,** 20, 22, 23, **26, 27, 29**
Warbling vireo	1, 7, 8, 9, 14, **17,** 27 (all of these are excellent for this bird)
Canada jay	**19** (check around the picnic area at the Echo Lake Trailhead)
Pinyon jay	28, 29, **30** (very itinerant and unpredictable)
Steller's jay	**1,** 4, 5, 11, **15, 19, 20,** 21, **22, 23,** 26, 27, **29** (common in coniferous forests)
Woodhouse's scrub-jay	8, 11, **16, 24, 25, 28,** 30
Clark's nutcracker	7, **19,** 21 (higher elevations up to tree line)
Mountain chickadee	Common on any of the foothills/mountain trails with coniferous forest
Juniper titmouse	28, 29, **30** (confined to the southern part of our area of interest)
Bushtit	1, **2, 8,** 14, 15, 17, **18,** 24, **25, 28,** 29, **30**
Nuthatches (including red-breasted and pygmy)	**1,** 4, 5, 11, **15,** 19, 20, 21, **22, 23, 26,** 27, **29**
White-breasted nuthatch	**1,** 3, 4, **8, 9,** 11, 13, **14, 15, 17,** 22, 23, **26,** 27, **29** (common in low-elevation deciduous woodlands and at higher elevations with the other nuthatches)
Brown creeper	same locations as red-breasted and pygmy nuthatches
Rock wren	**2, 8, 16,** 24, 25, 28
Canyon wren	**3, 8, 16,** 23, **24, 25,** 28
Marsh wren	**9, 12, 13**
Bewick's wren	**28, 29, 30** (occurs mostly at the southern end of our area of interest)
Blue-gray gnatcatcher	2, **8,** 11, 12, 13, 16, **17, 18, 25,** 27, **28,** 29, **30**
American dipper	**6,** 10, **14, 17, 18**

Kinglets (including golden-crowned and ruby-crowned)	5, **19**, **21**, 22, **23**, 26 (golden-crowned); 8, 9, 14, **17**, 22, 23, 24, 26 (ruby-crowned); look for golden-crowned at somewhat higher elevations and in more coniferous woodland
Hermit thrush	1, **6**, **19**, 21, **23**, 25, 26, 29
Bluebirds (including western and mountain)	2, 11, **15**, **16**, **18**, **20**, **23**, 25, 27, **29**, 30
Townsend's solitaire	1, 16, 18, 24, **25**, **27**, 28 (lower elevations in winter)
Gray catbird	**3**, 8, **14**, **17**, 18, **24**, 27
Sage thrasher	2, **8**, 12, 16, **18** (seen in the Front Range mostly in migration)
Cedar waxwing	**3**, 8, 13, 14, **17**, 27 (found in areas with good berry crop year round, flycatching over creeks in summer)
American pipit	**7** (S), **10** (W), 14 (W), 18 (W), **19** (S), **21** (S) (found along gravel stream banks in winter, above tree line in summer)
Mountain grosbeaks (including evening and pine grosbeaks)	1, 15, **19**, **21**, 23, **26** (these birds are itinerant [evening] and unpredictable [pine])
Rosy-finch (brown-capped in summer, plus black and gray-crowned in winter)	7 (especially Medicine Bow Curve, on snowfields), 20, 21 (upper lake)
Cassin's finch	1, 11, **15**, **21**, 22, **23**, **26**, 29 (mid- to high-elevation coniferous forests)
Red crossbill	same as Cassin's finch
Pine siskin	4, 8, 11, 17, 25 (same as Cassin's finch, but tend to wander a bit lower into deciduous woodlands)
Lesser goldfinch	**3**, 8, 11, **17**, 20, 24, 25
American goldfinch	2, **3**, 8, **9**, **12**, **13**, 14, **18**, 24, 27, 28 (anywhere there are weedy seed-bearing plants, especially thistle)
Grasshopper sparrow	**12**
Lark sparrow	**2**, **8**, **9**, **12**, **13**, 18, 24, 25, **28**, **29**, 30 (anywhere there are open, arid prairies)
Lark bunting	12
Chipping sparrow	1, 8, 9, **15**, 17, 22, 23, **26**, 29 (found on the plains during migration and nesting in foothills ponderosa forest in summer)
American tree sparrow	9, 10, **12**, 13, **14**, **18**, 28 (found in brushy habitat in winter only)

Lincoln's sparrow	**19**, **21**, 22 (found in mid- to high-elevation willow thickets in summer; shares this habitat with Wilson's and MacGillivray's warblers)
Canyon towhee	**28**, 29, **30** (occurs only in the southern part of our area of interest)
Green-tailed towhee	1, 2, **8**, **11**, **14**, **15**, 17, 18, 20, 22, 23, **25**, 26, 27, 28, 29 (occurs in summer in foothills with brushy habitat)
Spotted towhee	same as green-tailed towhee, but more likely to be seen in winter than green-tailed
Yellow-breasted chat	**3**, **8**, **11**, 18, **24**, 27 (similar to towhees but likes habitat that is somewhat more moist)
Bullock's oriole	3, 8, **9**, **10**, 12, **13**, **14**, 17, **18**, **24**, 25, 27 (any hike with low-elevation deciduous forest near water)
Virginia's warbler	8, 11, **17**, **24**, **25** (similar habitat as towhees)
MacGillivray's warbler	same as Lincoln's sparrow
Common yellowthroat	9, **12**, **13**, 14, 24 (occurs in summer in cattail marshes)
Yellow warbler	**1**, **3**, 8, **9**, **10**, 13, **14**, **17**, 18, **24**, 27 (any of our hikes that have low-elevation deciduous forest, especially near water)
Townsend's warbler	4, 8, 9, 10, 11, 13, 14, 18, 24, 27 (seen in fall migration on most of our hikes except very high elevation; somewhat sporadic)
Wilson's warbler	same as Lincoln's sparrow
Western tanager	**1**, 6, 11, **15**, **22**, **23**, 29 (found mostly in lower-elevation coniferous forests)
Black-headed grosbeak	1, 8, 9, 10, **11**, **13**, 14, **16**, **17**, **18**, **24**, **25**, 27, 28, 29, 30 (prefers lower-elevation deciduous woodland)
Blue grosbeak	1, **2**, **8**, **9**, **12**, 13, 18, 27, 28 (prairie specialist)
Lazuli bunting	1, 2, **3**, **8**, **11**, 13, 14, 16, **17**, 18, **24**, **25**, 27, 29

ABOUT THE AUTHOR

Norm grew up on the banks of the Ohio River in Clarksville, Indiana, where the Lewis (very distant relation) and Clark Expedition began (Skeptical? Check *Undaunted Courage* by Stephen Ambrose). It was in this area of abundant valleys, streams, and woodlands that he first developed an interest in all things natural, though birding, unfortunately, would not come until much later. He received a B.S. in geology from Indiana University, then went west to earn an M.S. in geology from Northern Arizona University at Flagstaff, Arizona. It was here that Norm began his hiking career. Not one for half measures, he cut his hiking teeth in the Grand Canyon.

Some years later, in 1984, Norm returned to Indiana to celebrate his mom's receiving her PhD from the University of Louisville. It being May, his brother Jerry inquired as to whether they might enjoy the spring migration together by doing some birding. "Some whating?" inquired Norm. "Birding," replied his brother. "You know, bird-watching." Always game for a new experience, he accompanied his brother into what passes for wilds in Indiana, and was hooked from the first bird (which happened to be a yellow warbler).

Upon returning to Denver, Norm became active in the birding community, eventually serving as president of the Denver Field Ornithologists and Colorado Field Ornithologists. He became associated with the Denver Museum of Nature and Science as a volunteer field trip leader, and upon retirement was hired by the museum, leading birding field trips and tours and teaching beginning birding classes. He has been working with the museum since 1993. Norm has also been hosting seminars on birding for the Colorado Mountain Club.

In his thirty-six years of birding (at this writing), Norm has developed a passion not only for all things birding, but also for sharing his passion with other aspiring birders. It is with great pleasure and satisfaction that he presents this guidebook, in the hope that it will help encourage some other outdoor enthusiast to expand their interest in birding. He further hopes that this interest may grow and that birding may provide a lifetime of learning and entertainment, and the enjoyment of wild things in wild places.

Norm Lewis

Recreate with
RIMS

Give back to the land you love with the CMC RIMS (Recreation Impact Monitoring System) mobile app: If you spot a downed tree, trail erosion, trash, or poor signage while you're exploring the places in this book, open the app and submit a quick report so that land managers can address the issue. Learn more and get started at www.cmc.org/RIMS.

www.cmc.org/RIMS

Illustration by Jesse Crock

Join Today.
Adventure Tomorrow.

The Colorado Mountain Club is the Rocky Mountain community for mountain education, adventure, and conservation. We bring people together to share our love of the mountains. We value our community and go out of our way to welcome and include all Coloradoans—from the uninitiated to the expert, there is a place for everyone here.

COLORADO MOUNTAIN CLUB · SINCE 1912

www.cmc.org